9/5/22

TREKKING ING IN
NORTHERN SPAIN

ILJA SCHRÖDER AND JIM THOMSON

Climbing consultant VICTOR SAUNDERS

**NEW
HOLLAND**

First published in 2003 by
New Holland Publishers (UK) Ltd
London · Cape Town · Sydney · Auckland

Garfield House, 86–88 Edgware Road,
London W2 2EA, United Kingdom

80 McKenzie Street, Cape Town 8001, South Africa

14 Aquatic Drive, Frenchs Forest, NSW 2086, Australia

218 Lake Road, Northcote, Auckland, New Zealand

www.newhollandpublishers.com

2 4 6 8 10 9 7 5 3 1

Publishing Manager: Jo Hemmings
Series Editor: Kate Michell
Assistant Editors: Jessica Cowie, Anne Konopelski
Design: Gülen Shevki
Cartography: William Smuts
Production: Lucy Hulme, Joan Woodroffe

Reproduction by Modern Age Repro Co. Ltd, Hong Kong
Printed and bound by Kyodo Printing Co (Singapore) Pte Ltd

The author and publisher have made every effort to ensure
that the information in this book was correct when the
book went to press; they accept no responsibility for any
loss, injury or inconvenience sustained by any person using
this book.

Front cover: The mountain range of Los Alanos near Zuriza
forms a spectacular backdrop to the Upper Veral valley
(trek 8). *Cover spine:* Snow-shoe walking in the Spanish
Alaska (trek 11). *Title page:* An old shepherd's hut built
in the traditional Celtic style of the Picos de Europa
(Chapter 7). *This spread:* As the early morning mist from
the nearby lakes clears the rocky terrain of Covadonga is
revealed (trek 13). *Opposite contents page:* The lush surroundings of the Upper Río del Freser (trek 1). *Contents
page top:* Glacial rivers have cut their way through the landscape of northern Spain (trek 5); *upper middle:* The rare
Brown bear is still to be found in the region's more remote
forests (trek 8); *lower middle:* Ramshackle wooden bridges
enable trekkers to cross fast-flowing rivers (trek 5); *bottom:*
The evening sun gives a warm glow to the jagged peaks of
Pico de los Cabrones (trek 15).

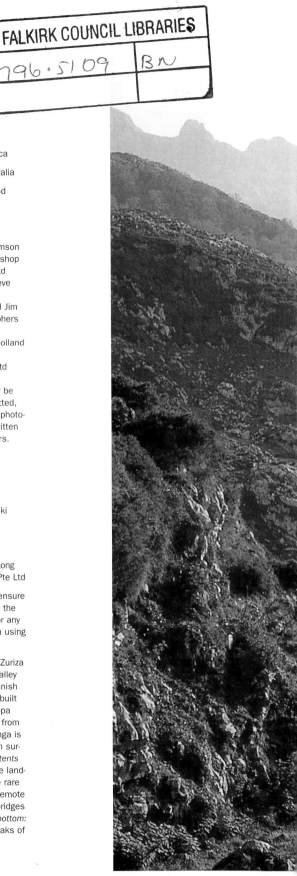

CONTENTS

ABOUT THIS BOOK

Covering the north of Spain from east to west, this book is divided into five chapters: the Eastern (Catalunian) Pyrenees, the Western (Aragones–Navarro) Pyrenees, the Cordillera Cantábrica, the Picos de Europa and, finally, a chapter dedicated to a single route, the famous El Camino de Santiago, which runs across the breadth of northern Spain. Each chapter gives in-depth coverage of a number of recommended trekking routes, plus selected climbing peaks that can be reached from the treks.

Like the trekking routes themselves, the peaks featured range in difficulty (from an easy scramble to a moderately technical climb) but mostly fall well within the horizon of any properly equipped and experienced party. They are presented as a natural highpoint of trekking in a mountainous region.

Three introductory sections precede the regional chapters. An opening chapter provides a brief snapshot of northern Spain, its geography, people and culture. The second chapter provides all the practical advice you should need on arrival in the country and for travel to the various regions; while the third covers all the practicalities thereafter – the logistics of setting off on a trek and the possible extra requirements that may be involved in climbing peaks en route.

Regional directories at the end of each chapter consolidate the general advice given in the introductory sections with specific listings information.

Appendices on the mountain environment, mountain photography and health and safety for trekkers complete the book.

LEGEND

A9	Motorway		✈	Airport/airstrip
N550 / tunnel	Highway		⬤	Mountain hut
	Provincial road		⌂	Mountain hut unmanned
	Secondary road		⚑	Cabin
	Track/footpath		☼	Viewpoint
alternative route	Trek route		▲	Campsite
	Peak route		Collado de Añisclo	Mountain pass
	International boundary		Monte Perdido ▲ 3355m (11008ft)	Peak in metres (feet)
	Railway		Glaciar de Monte Perdido	Glacier
▢ BARCELONA	City		dam / river	Water features
◉ PONTEVEDRA	Major town			Altitude contour (2000m/6562ft on trek maps)
○ Ripoll	Town			Ridge
◎ Berga	Small town		PARET NORD	Mountain range
○ Saldes	Village/building/ruin		❶ ❶	Trek number
✈	International airport			Cable car/chairlift

Trek Essentials boxes summarize each trek, including approximate number of days required, means of access to the start of the trek, highest elevations reached, trekking style involved and official restrictions, if any. Also mentioned are notable variations on the route.

Top-class **mapping** pinpoints the route of each trek, with ridge lines, selected altitude contours, glaciers, passes and nearest roads included. Also illustrated in dotted lines are alternative trails and in blue lines are access routes to peaks.

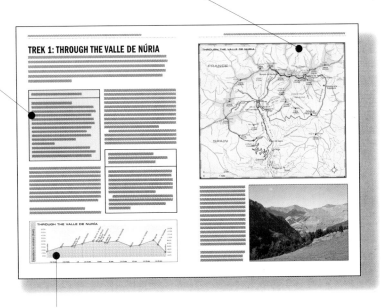

Strip maps illustrate the elevation profile of each trek, including key passes and spot heights, as well as walking times. (NB: Strip maps are illustrative and not designed for cross-reference between treks.)

Climb Essentials boxes summarize the characteristics of each climbing route, including summit height, principal camps and grade of climb.

Specially sourced **topo photographs** show the general approach route to each climbing peak, with the route clearly marked in red. A dotted line indicates where the route goes behind the mountain face shown.

1

INTRODUCTION TO NORTHERN SPAIN

An often overlooked part of the glorious country that is Spain is the lush yet rugged terrain of the north. An area bursting with history, the ancient kingdoms of Asturias, Navarra, Aragón, Galicia, Castile and León have left their mark on the area through both legends and historical buildings.

Although a relatively small region, it is nevertheless wonderfully diverse, particularly in culture, dialect and lifestyle – from regions with an industrial mining past to untouched rural idylls where self-sufficiency was once the order of the day. The landscape is equally abundant in variety, with snowcapped mountains towering over surging rivers, ravines and peaceful flower-filled pastures.

Mountain ponies can be found roaming the hillsides of northern Spain. Although not wild, these creatures are still left to fend for themselves for much of the year.

The snow-covered peak of Peña Prieta reflected in a mountain stream is a reminder of the year-round beauty of the Cordillera Cantábrica (trek 11).

THE SPANISH CLIMATES

The Iberian peninsula's geographical conditions have caused it to become one of the most varied biospheres of Europe – from the southern flanks of the Pyrenees down to the plains of the Río Ebro, the climate changes from alpine to sub-desert – with an unbeatable wealth of flora and fauna.

It is possible to divide the peninsula into three different climatic zones. The northern side of the Cordillera Cantábrica is subject to a moist Atlantic climate, which consists of damp and moderate summers with rainy, mild winters. With an average precipitation in the hills of between 800–3000mm (30–120in) per year, it's no wonder that the area is known as Green Spain by the tourist brochures. In summer, the humidity from the nearby Atlantic Ocean builds up and condenses as fog along the northern side of the mountains. This weather pattern also affects the French Pyrenees, which are fundamentally rainier than those on the sunny Spanish side. As a consequence of this moist climate, one finds romantic valleys filled with extensive lush forests and roaring brooks and rivers.

On the southern side of the Cordillera and the Pyrenees the climate, landscape and vegetation change abruptly. Here, the climate is typically continental, with relatively dry and sometimes bitterly cold winters and hot parched summers. From approximately November to March, large parts of Spain suffer from the influence of the rainy Atlantic weather, while the summer months enjoy high-pressure systems from the Azores. The landscape south of the Cordillera and the Pyrenees is shaped mainly by farming, with corn being the main crop, while the barren karst foothills are used for grazing cattle, goat and sheep.

A large portion of the southern half of Spain, stretching from around the province of Madrid southwards (known as the southern Meseta or New Castilla), comes under the influence of a Mediterranean climate, with muggy winters and dry hot summers – the summer temperatures can soar to over 45°C (113°F) inland. Since Roman times, large areas of forest have been cleared for timber production, leaving a prairie similar in char-

THE LAND

In my opinion the north of Spain is one of the most beautiful and varied landscapes of Europe. Few are aware that, after Switzerland, Spain is the most mountainous country in Europe, with more than 80 per cent of the country lying higher than 800m (2600ft) above sea level.

The mountain ranges of the Cordillera Cantábrica and the Pyrenees dominate northern Spain. These alpine rocky massifs with their wide valleys, which separate the arid plateau of the Meseta (which runs south of the Cordillera Cantábrica across most of central Spain) from the 'Green Coast' (La Costa Verde) and France, are noted for their inaccessibility. This seclusion has resulted in both the countryside and people retaining their individuality. Many ancient social and agricultural customs have survived and contribute to the beauty of the landscape.

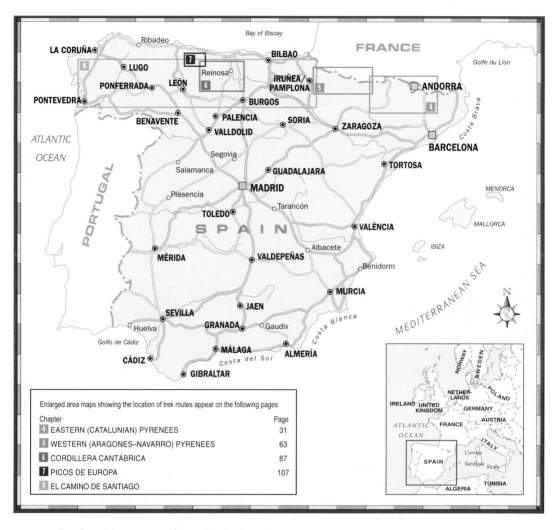

acter to that found in western Africa. The 'Dahesa', or traditional pasture, is interspersed with oak trees whose acorns are used for feeding the famous Iberian pigs. Sadly, only a few of the original Mediterranean woods still exist today. However, due to their ecological importance, these woods are now heavily protected.

POLITICAL HISTORY

Since Spanish unification in 1492 until the beginning of the 20th century Spain had always been a monarchy. Its last king, Alfonso XIII, exiled himself when the dictator Primo de Ribera rose to power in 1923.

After Ribera's assassination in 1926 a free election resulted in the first Spanish Republic. However, on 18 July 1936, under the command of General Mola, a military coup was held. Only a few days later Mola was killed in an aircraft acci-

dent and command passed to General Franco. A fierce civil war was fought between the Republicans and the Nationalists. The Republicans were eventually defeated in 1939. Franco remained in power for 36 years and spent his last few years grooming the young Juan Carlos (Prince of Asturias) to be his successor, as he feared the legitimate heir to the throne, Don Juan, would not continue with his ideologies.

After Franco's death in 1975, King Juan Carlos became Head of State and surprised the nation by instigating a return to democracy. During this period many exiled politicians returned to Spain and their various parties were declared legal, the last of which was the PCE (Partido Comunista de España) led by Santiago Carrillo and Dolores Ibarruri, also known as 'La Pasionaria'.

In 1976 Adolfo Suarez was named prime minister by the King and in the same year there

Unlike in the south of the country, bullfights in Northern Spain are generally bloodless.

was a political referendum in which 94 per cent of the electorate were in favour of political reform. In 1977 the first general election took place and Suarez's party, the Union of Democratic Centre (UCD), gained victory. The Spanish Constitution of 1978 recognized and guaranteed the rights of autonomy to the 17 regions within the Spanish State, and in March 1980 the first autonomous elections were held.

Spain gained full entry to the EEC in 1992, and now, with its distinct parliaments, each self-governing such things as health, education, tax, etc., it has left behind its political isolation to truly become a member of the modern European community.

CUSTOMS AND TRADITIONS

Spain has cultivated customs and traditions unlike any other European country. Many of the rituals carried out during the fiestas date back to the Middle Ages and often have religious undertones. Processions carrying an effigy of the Virgin Mary or

local patron saint through the narrow streets of the towns and villages, accompanied by countless euphoric supporters, are a common feature of fiestas. It is after the procession, however, that is the most important part of the fiesta for old and young alike, as this is when the music, dancing and drinking start. The next day has often dawned by the time the celebrations have ended.

Each village has a patron saint, and almost every street or *barrio* celebrates its own fiesta. Practically anything can be cause for celebration – livestock markets, the end of the fishing season, the 'day of the cheese' or the *fiesta del vino* (festival of wine) are not uncommon reasons for merriment.

Many fiestas in the north of Spain have heathen and Celtic rituals. Usually, the young dress up and change the village street into a scene from the Dark Ages when goblins, witches, and dark powers were believed to dominate the mountains and valleys. For these celebrations the *gaita*, a type of bagpipe typical of the northern coastal region, is one of the most important musical instruments.

To the horror of many outsiders, Spanish rituals often involve the slaughtering of wild and domestic animals. However, increasingly strong criticism from the Spanish themselves, especially within the younger generations, has seen changes – in particular, domestic animals are no longer abused in rituals.

In many cultures the killing of wild animals is traditionally considered a sign of manliness and heroism; this is true of Spanish bullfighting. The north and south of Spain differ in many cultural, as well as geographical, respects, but especially so in the controversial bullfight. In the north, except in the Navarra and Rioja regions, bullfighting is not so important. While in the south, the bullfight (*corrida*) is not only an important celebration, but is also regarded as a blend of art and philosophy. Bullfighters (*Toreros*) are respected artists, not unlike musicians or painters. It seems that with each survived goring (*cornada*) the young men and, more recently, women become more renowned. Ironically, the only bulls that survive the *corrida* are those that ignore the derogatory whistles from the audience and refuse to fight.

Bullfights are always accompanied by music from the local band.

Another tradition, but no less exhausting for men and hoofed animals alike, is the migration of livestock, the *Trashumancia*. Each year, thousands of sheep and cattle journey over more than 800km (480 miles) of Spanish countryside, from the dry hot south to the green pastures of the north (and back), in search of summer grazing. In order not to lose their right of transit, this centuries-old tradition still involves the herding of over 2,000 sheep through the very centre of Spain's capital city, Madrid.

PYRENEAN DESMAN

The Pyrenean desman (*Galemys pyrenaicus*) is a type of mole found throughout the whole of the northern Cordillera. Highly aquatic in nature, it – along with Russian desmans – possesses paddle-like hind feet, which are wider than its forefeet, and an extremely long tail.

Adept swimmers and accomplished divers, Pyrenean desmans primarily forage for food by sifting through stream sediments with their forefeet and long bi-lobed snout in search of aquatic insects. While chiefly nocturnal in habit, these amphibious mammals also exhibit short periods of activity during the day, so you may just be lucky enough to spot one.

2

ARRIVING IN
NORTHERN
SPAIN

The proximity of Santander, Bilbao and Madrid to the regions covered in this book allows for numerous ways of reaching Spain itself and for continuing your trip within. You may wish to absorb the culture of the country by using public transport or prefer the freedom that a hired car gives you – whichever you choose you will be sure to be privy to some of the most beautiful landscapes in Europe.

Although a trip to Northern Spain will not test you in the same way as a trip to the Patagonian Andes or an expedition to the Himalaya might, the different languages, dialects, food and basic public transportation systems may all cause confusion. Hence, this chapter will aim to guide you through the basics of travel in Spain.

The rack and pinion railway climbs some 800m (2625ft) through the rugged countryside to reach the former monastery at Núria (trek 1).

VISAS

Visitors from EU countries are only required to carry their National Identity Card or passport to enter Spain. Visas are also unnecessary for US citizens, Australians and New Zealanders, all of whom will receive authorization for a three-month stay on entry to Spain.

Visitors from elsewhere are required to apply for visas from the Spanish consulate in their place of domicile before setting off.

SPANISH TIME AND OPENING HOURS

The Spanish mainland is one hour ahead of Greenwich Mean Time (GMT) in winter and two hours ahead of GMT in summer.

Although Spain is in the far west of Europe it still uses Central European time. This has the consequence that the sun rises and sets quite late in the day. Generally, Spaniards are not early risers, and public life seldom starts before 9am.

Particularly important is the famous 'siesta' – businesses and public offices are usually closed between 2pm and 5pm. During siesta time the streets are more or less extinct of life, especially in the south where the afternoon heat is often unbearable. It is advisable to follow the example of the locals and spend the siesta in the cool and shade.

Towards evening everything re-opens. Spain has no laws regarding business hours, so it remains more or less up to each individual business as to what time to close. In the summer months some shops and businesses are still open until very late at night and, in turn, dinner is normally taken between 10pm and 11pm. Bars and discos stay open until the early hours.

MONEY

The Spanish currency is now the euro, which circulates in coins of 1, 2, 5, 10, 20, 50 cents and

SPANISH EMBASSIES OVERSEAS

Australia: 15 Arkana St, Yarralumba, ACT 2600; POB 9076, Deakin, ACT 2600 Canberra
Tel.: +61-2-6273-3555 Fax: +61-2-6273-3918
Canada: 74 Stanley Avenue, Ottawa (Ontario), K1M 1P4, Ottawa
Tel.: +1-613-747-2252 Fax: +1-613-744-1224
Denmark: Upsalagade 26, 2100 Copenhagen
Tel.: +45-31-42-47-00 Fax: +45-35-26-30-99
France: 22 Avenue Marceau, 75381 Paris, Cédex 08, Paris
Tel.: +33-144-43-18-00 Fax: +33-147-20-56-69
Germany: Schöneberger Ufer, 89 10785 Berlin
Tel.: +49-302-54-00-70 Fax: +49-302-57-99-557
Ireland: 17A Merlyn Park, Ballsbridge, Dublin 4
Tel.: +353-1-269-16-40 Fax: +353-1-269-18-54
Italy: Palacio Borghese, Lardo Fontanella di Borghese 19, 00186 Rome
Tel.: +39-6-687-82-64 Fax: +39-6-687-22-56
Netherlands: Lange Voorhout 50, 2514 EG The Hague
Tel.: +31-70-364-38-14 Fax: +31-70-361-79-59
South Africa: 169 Pine St, Arcadia, Pretoria 0083
Tel.: +27-12-344-38-75 Fax: +27-12-343-48-91
Sweden: 10055 Stockholm o/y Djurgârdsvägen 21, Djurgârden, 15 21 Stockholm
Tel.: +46-8-667-94-30 Fax: +46-8-663-79-65
Switzerland: Kalcheggweg 24, 3000 Bern 16
Tel.: +41-31-352-04-12 Fax: +41-31-351-52-29
UK: 39 Chesham Place, London SW1X 8SB
Tel.: +44-171-235-55-55 Fax: +44-171-259-53-92
USA: 2375 Pennsylvania Avenue N.W., Washington DC 20037
Tel.: +1-202-452-0100 Fax: +1-202-833-5670

INTERNATIONAL EMBASSIES IN SPAIN

Australia: Plaza Del Descubridor Diego de Ordás 3, 28003 Madrid
Tel.: +34 91-441-93-00 Fax: +34 91-442-53-62
Canada: C/Núñez de Balboa 35, 28001 Madrid
Tel.: +34 91-431-43-00 Fax: +34 91-431-23-67
Denmark: C/Claudio Coello 91, 4°, 28006 Madrid
Tel.: +34 91-431-84-45 Fax: +34 91-431-91-68
France: C/Salustiano Olózaga 9, 28001 Madrid
Tel.: +34 91-423-89-00 Fax: +34 91-423-89-01
Germany: C/Fortuny 8, 28001 Madrid
Tel.: +34 91-557-90-00 Fax: +34 91-310-21-04
Ireland: Paso de la Castellana 36, 28046 Madrid
Tel.: +34 91-576-35-00 Fax: +34 91-435-16-77
Italy: C/Lagasca 98, 28006 Madrid
Tel.: +34 91-577- 65-29 Fax: +34 91-575-77-76
Netherlands: Avda Comandante Franco 32, 28016 Madrid
Tel.: +34 91-359-09-14 Fax: +34 91-359-21-50
New Zealand: Plaza de la Lealtad 2, 3°, 28014 Madrid
Tel.: +34 91-523-02-26 Fax: +34 91-523-01-71
South Africa: C/Claudio Coello 91, 6° y 7°, 28006 Madrid
Tel.: +34 91-436-37-80 Fax: +34 91-577-74-14
Sweden: C/Caracas 25, 28010 Madrid
Tel.: +34 91-308-15-35 Fax: +34 91-308-19-03
Switzerland: C/Núñez de Balboa 35, 7°, 28001 Madrid
Tel.: +34 91-436-39-60 Fax: +34 91-436-39-80
UK: C/Fernando el Santo 16, 28010 Madrid
Tel.: +34 91-700-82-00 Fax: +34 91-700-82-10
USA: C/Serrano 75, 28006 Madrid
Tel.: +34 91-587-22-00 Fax: +34 91-587-23-03

INTERNATIONAL AIRLINES

Iberia: 020 7830 0011 (UK); 800-892-4141 (USA);
www.iberia.com
British Airways: 0845 7733377 (UK); www.britishairways.com
GB Airways: 0845 7733377 (UK); www.britishairways.com
Go Airlines: 0845 6054321 (UK); www.go-fly.com
Easy Jet: 0870 6000000 (UK); www.easyjet.com
TWA: 800-892-4141 (USA); www.twa.com
Delta Airlines: 800-241-4141 (USA); www.delta.com
Continental Airlines: 800-231-0856 (USA);
www.continental.com

1 and 2 euros, and notes of 5, 10, 20 and 50, 100, 200, 500 euros.

Banks and *cajas de ahorro* (equivalent to a building society or savings and loan company) have branches in most towns; their hours are Monday to Friday 9am–2pm, Saturday 9am–1pm. Cash can also be changed at larger hotels, with travel agents in the cities and big resorts and at *casas de cambio* (bureaux de change). ATM machines are widespread throughout Spain.

TRAVEL TO AND IN SPAIN
NB: All public transport in Spain is drastically reduced on Sundays and holidays, and it is best to avoid travelling to out-of-the-way places on these days (see page 21).

By air
The most favourable and fastest way of reaching the Iberian peninsula is by air. Innumerable airline companies fly to Bilbao, Madrid and Barcelona. Internal flights can then be taken to smaller airports, such as Oviedo, Santander, Pamplona or Zaragoza.

By boat
A practical but costly way of reach the north of Spain from the UK is by ferry. P&O ferries operate a service from Portsmouth to Bilbao (36 hours) and Brittany ferries run a service from Plymouth to Santander (23 hours). The advantage of taking the ferry is that you can take your own car.

By car
From the UK, you can drive through France all the way to Spain. Recently, the French and Spanish road network has been vastly

improved and Spain can be reached from the UK in a day's (albeit a long day) drive. Be aware, however, that in the more remote areas petrol stations are sparse and are not normally open 24 hours.

If a long drive even before you have started on your adventure sounds tiresome, a good alternative is to hire a car on your arrival by boat or plane. A car will undoubtedly give you a lot of freedom. Hire cars are readily available in all major towns and airports, but it is usually cheaper to arrange car rental from your home country.

Major roads are generally good and traffic is calm on the whole. Speed limits are 50–60kph in built-up areas, 120kph on highways and 90–100kph on other roads. If you need breakdown assistance, road-side phones on major routes are connected to the local police station which will arrange assistance; on minor routes contact the nearest police station via the operator.

Not all sections of the treks pass through glorious countryside. Here, two modern-day pilgrims on El Camino de Santiago leave León (trek 16).

By train

The train is a relatively cheap and reliable medium of transport in Spain. However, it is notoriously slow, particularly in the more remote regions. Not only is the journey to Spain from abroad marked by frequent changes, long stays and waiting periods, but travel within the country can be very time-consuming. Nevertheless, the local train lines do pass through extraordinary scenery, which you will be able to fully appreciate.

RENFE, the Spanish rail company, operates a variety of train services. An ordinary train, much the same speed and cost as the bus, will be described as an *expreso*, *regional* or *rápido*. Semi-*directos*, *tranvías* (mostly short-haul) and *correos* (mail trains) are slower. Expresses, which vary greatly in expense, are known as Delta, Intercity TER, Talgo and Talgo 2000.

Tickets can be bought at the train station, but also at travel agents that display the RENFE sign and at RENFE offices in town centres. RENFE rail passes are available and seem to be accepted on all trains.

By bus

Another cheap and reliable form of transport are coaches. During the summer they connect most major and smaller towns to each other. Many smaller villages are accessible only by bus, almost always leaving from the capital of their province. Most bus companies are privately owned and run a cheap daily scheduled service. Service varies in quality, but the buses are reliable and comfortable enough, and it is an environmentally friendly way to travel around Spain. Many towns have no main station, and buses may leave from a variety of places – ask in the local tourist office or any bar.

By taxi

A more recent development in Spanish transport is the private taxi company. Private taxis are not particularly cheap, but serve a useful purpose in inaccessible areas. Many taxis are all-terrain vehicles suitable for travelling to the starting point of a walk or back to the next town or village.

ACCOMMODATION
Paradors

Paradors are luxury hotels and were first created in 1923 by King Alfonso XIII at the suggestion of the Marques de la Vega Inclán to restore historic buildings that were abandoned or going to ruin. Normally located in remote areas and converted from monasteries, castles, abbeys or country

These traditional grain stores, known as 'horreos', are a typical feature of the landscape of Asturias.

houses, they offer exceptional quality in both décor and service. At present there are 86 paradors throughout Spain.

Hotels
Hotels can be found in most villages throughout Spain and are rated from one- to five-star. The star rating is a reference to each hotel's facilities, and does not indicate the quality of service or décor. Therefore, a one-star or two-star hotel might be cheaper, better decorated and more friendly than a nearby four-star hotel.

Pensions
Pensions are similar to hotels, but often slightly more basic – the rooms may be smaller and without en-suite facilities.

Casas Rurales
A *casa rurale* is a traditional private house with rooms to let. They serve breakfast, but not evening meals.

Albergues
Albergues offer the cheapest form of lodging. They are bunkhouses located in villages or remote areas. Sleeping accommodation is shared, and most have more than four beds per room. There is at least one bathroom per six beds.

Refuges
Refuges are run by various mountaineering federations and are similar to *albergues* but are located in isolated mountain areas. They may or may not have water or toilets. Sleeping is normally

In late autumn the countryside is set alight by the changing hues of the indigenous trees and bushes.

in a communal dormitory. Basic meals are often available. Many are only manned during the summer months. Unmanned refuges are normally smaller with no facilities, including no beds.

Campsites
Campsites are found in almost all villages and towns. The facilities they offer vary considerably from one location to the next.

Wild camping (bivouacking)
The law on camping wild on public land in Spain is quite complicated. It is prohibited to camp by the side of a road or within 500m (1640ft) of a river, and the tent has to be taken down every day. In the national parks, rules vary from one location to the next, but usually, above 1600m (5250ft), tents can be erected one hour before sunset and dismantled one hour after sunrise. It's best to ask in the nearest park office regarding the specific rules that apply to each park.

FOOD
Spain, with its rich variety of specialities, is a fantastic country for food-lovers. This gastro-

---

SPANISH WINE

Spanish wines fall into five distinct categories and are controlled by a government regulatory body for each wine-producing region (Denominación de Origen Controlee/DOC):

1. *Vino de mesa* – 'table wine'.

2. *Vino joven* – 'young wine'; usually from a qualified DOC region, often with a bit of ageing, but not old enough to be a 'crianza'.

3. *Crianza* – 'mature wine'; aged for two years, with at least six months in an oak cask.

4. *Reserva* – 'quality wine'; at least one year in an oak cask and two years in the bottle; made from top vintages.

5. *Gran Reserva* – 'high quality wine'; at least two to three years in an oak cask, plus three years in the bottle; made from exceptional vintages.

SPANISH WORDS AND PHRASES

EVERYDAY PHRASES

Hola	OH-la	Hello
Buenos días	BWEHnohs DEEahs	Good morning
Buenas tardes	BWEHnahs TARdehs	Good afternoon
Adiós	ahdeeOHS	Goodbye
Buenas noches	BWEHnahs NOchehs	Good night
Gracias	GRAtheeahs	Thank you
De nada	deh NAdah	Not at all
Por favor	por fahVOR	Please
Oiga	OYga	(formal, to call attention)
Perdón	PairDOHN	Sorry, pardon
No importa	Noh imPORtah	It doesn't matter
Sí/No	See/Noh	Yes/No
Bien	BeeEHN	Fine, well
Vale	VAHlay	All right
¿Qué?/¿Cómo?	¿Keh?/COHmoh?	What?/Sorry?
¿A qué hora?	¿Ah keh OHrah?	What time?

EATING & SHOPPING

Para comer	Pahrah cohMEHR	for a meal
Para beber	Pahrah behBEHR	for a drink
Agua	AHgwah	water
Zumo	THUmoh	juice
Café	cahFAY	coffee
Té	Teh	tea
Cerveza	therVAYthah	beer
Caña	CAnya	draught
Vino	VEEnoh	wine
Tinto/blanco	TEENtoh/BLANcoh	red/white
Carne	CARneh	meat
Pescado	pesCAHdoh	fish
Verdura	verDOOrah	vegetables
Fruta	FROOtah	fruit
Pan	pahn	bread
Sólo verdura	SOHloh verDOOrah	only vegetables
Soy vegetariano/a	Soy veh-hehtahreeAnoh	I'm vegetarian
(No) me gusta	(Noh) meh GOOstah	I (don't) like
Me da... por favor	Meh dah... por fahVOR	Please give me...
¿Cuánto es?	¿KWANtoh ehs?	How much is (it)?
Euros	EHoorohs	euros
Céntimos	THEHNteemohs	cents
Médico	MEHdeecoh	doctor
Farmacia	farMAHtheeah	pharmacy
Abierto	ahbeeEHRtoh	open
Cerrado	thehRAHdoh	closed

WEATHER

¿El tiempo para mañana?	¿Ell teeEMpoh pahrah mahNYAnah?	The weather for tomorrow?
Sol	sohl	sun, sunny
Nubes/nublado	NOObehs/nooBLAHdoh	clouds/cloudy
Lluvia	YOOveeah	rain
Tormenta	torMENtah	storm
Nieve	neeEHveh	snow
Hielo	EEAYloh	ice
Viento	veeEHNtoh	wind, windy
Niebla	neeEHblah	fog
Calor	cahLOR	hot
Frío	FREEoh	cold
Buen tiempo	bwehn teeEMpoh	fair weather
Mal tiempo	mahl teeEMpo	bad weather
Temperatura	tempehrahTOOrah	temperature
Grados	GRAHdohs	degrees
Mucho	MOOchoh	many, a lot
Poco	POHcoh	few, a little

TRAVELLING AROUND

Estación	estahtheeOHN	station
Aeropuerto	ahehrohPWERtoh	airport
Taxi	TAKsee	taxi
Coche de alquiler	COHcheh deh alkeeLEHR	hired car
Hotel	ohTEL	hotel
Habitación	ahbeetahtheeOHN	room
Doble	DOHbleh	double
Simple	SIMpleh	single
Una noche	OOnah NOHcheh	one night
Dónde está...?	¿DOHNdeh esTAH... ?	Where is... ?
Aquí	ahKEE	here
Ahí	ahEE	over there
Cerca	THERkah	near
Lejos	LEHhohs	far
Senda	SENdah	footpath
Pista	PEEStah	jeep track
Camino	cahMEEnoh	way
Carretera	carehTEHrah	tarmac road
Sube	SOObeh	go up, ascend
Baja	BAH-hah	go down, descend
Rápido	RAHpeedoh	fast
Lento	LENtoh	slow
Mapa	MAHpah	map
Caminar	cahmeeNAR	walking

nomic wealth may be due to the difference in landscape and culture between the north and south, on the other hand it might be due to the influence of other Mediterranean cultures, such as the Romans or Arabs.

Most regional dishes involve quality local ingredients and relatively simple preparation. In the mountainous north people prefer fatty meat dishes served with chips, while in the south a low-fat Mediterranean diet with many salads and vegetables predominant. The country's long tradition of fishing means that seafood dishes are to be found everywhere, especially along the coast. Madrid, despite its distance from the sea, has some of the finest seafood restaurants in Europe.

The best known 'tourist dish' is paella, a rice and seafood platter which originates from the Mediterranean region of Valencia. In the big cities, you'll find every type of regional cuisine available. The Basque country is particularly renowned for its cuisine, and in cities like Bilbao, San Sebastián and Pamplona specialities such as *merluza* (hake) or *bacalao* (cod) are regarded as being among the finest in the country.

Wine and tapas

Contrary to common belief, Spain and not France is the biggest producer of wine in the world. The best known are the quality reds from Rioja and Ribera del Duero, reds and whites from Penedés, fine whites from Rueda, 'sherries' from Jerez and cava, Spain's equivalent of champagne, from Catalunia. Approximately 60 per cent of wine production is consumed within the country, with the rest being exported.

One of the country's favourite pastimes is to stop in the local bars for a glass of *tinto* (red wine) washed down with *pinchos* (nibbles) or *tapas* (small portions) before returning home for the evening meal. These snacks range in quality and price across the country, sometimes they are free while in other places a small charge is made.

ELECTRICITY

The electric current is 220 volts and standard European sockets are used everywhere. For people travelling from the UK, plug adapters can be purchased in all major airports and on all cross-channel ferries.

COMMUNICATIONS

You can make international phonecalls direct from any phone box marked *teléfono internacional* or from Telecom offices. The operator number is 1004 for domestic calls, 025 for international information. The international access code is 07, then dial the country code followed by the local number.

HOLIDAYS

There are 14 national holidays: January 1; January 6; Good Friday; Easter Sunday and Monday; May 1; Corpus Christi (early or mid-June); June 24; July 25; August 15; October 12; November 1; December 6; December 8; December 25.

In addition to these are numerous local and regional holidays.

LANGUAGE

To get the best out of any trip abroad, learning at least a few key phrases is invaluable, as well as learning how to pronounce the alphabet and spell out your own name. In Northern Spain, do not be daunted by the fact that there are four main language groups spoken – Castilian, Basque, Catalan and Gallego – plus numerous dialects, as everyone speaks and understands Castilian (aka Spanish), which is the language that Spanish phrase-books employ.

Traditional farming methods are still practised in many of the rural areas.

3

TREKKING AND CLIMBING IN

NORTHERN SPAIN

The well-marked footpaths of the Pyrenees, Cordillera Cantábrica and Picos de Europa are gateways to unforgettable panoramic views and a natural history extravanganza with everything from chamoix to bears, alpine flowers to gigantic forests and birds of prey aplenty soaring the thermals above you.

Although the paths are waymarked, as in any mountainous environment, care must always be exercised and trekkers should consider the issues covered in the following chapter, as well as always carry a relevant map, compass and emergency provisions in case of the unexpected.

During the winter months large portions of the Pyrenees, including Peñaforca, are covered in deep snow (trek 8).

ACCOMMODATION

It was only a few years ago that this area of Europe was 'discovered' by foreign visitors. This new influx has led to on-going improvement of the infrastructure of local towns and municipalities. Today, it is no longer difficult to find a hotel, or at least an *albergue* (bunkhouse) in most villages.

Nevertheless, after many years of trekking and exploring these lonely mountains, I still feel it is necessary to warn against the dangers of going unprepared into what remains a harsh environment.

From the end of October to Easter almost all of the refuges and campsites in the mountains are closed. Only a handful of refuges stay open throughout the year to provide food and shelter to cold and hungry hikers. In the summer, the refuges get very busy and without a reservation you might have to be content with just a hard wooden bunk, or even the floor, to sleep on – it is always worth booking in advance.

At the end of each chapter contact information for refuges and tourist information is provided, but even so, the unexpected can always occur. In the course of researching this book, after a long and hard day I made my way towards what was, to me, a well-known refuge. Imagine my surprise as I found only the charred remains of a once spacious and comfortable refuge. The only solution was to bivouac for the night and try to make myself as comfortable as possible. Fortunately, I had the supplies on me to make this possible, but I've often met ill-equipped and inexperienced hikers who have escaped tragedy only by luck.

CLOTHING AND EQUIPMENT

As mentioned in previous chapters, Spain is not always the sun-drenched land that everyone imagines, and the mountainous areas can be subject to often extreme weather fluctuations. It is not unusual for a lovely sunny day to turn, within a few hours or even minutes, to winter conditions. Nor is it the exception to find snow and ice underfoot as late as June – it is particularly important in the Pyrenees and Picos de Europa to carry crampons and an ice-axe.

For this reason, all treks should be well planned and prepared for. It is essential that you carry the appropriate clothing and equipment for the time of year, and it is equally important to be fully aware of the conditions (especially in winter with the risk of avalanches) you are likely to be trekking in. Always respect the mountains.

Boots One of the most important pieces of equipment for hikers are well-fitting boots. These should have good Vibram-type soles and ankle support. It is important that boots should be well worn in before you start on a trek in order to avoid rub points and painful blisters.

Clothing Applying the layer system is strongly recommended. Several thin fibre-pile T-shirts, a fleece jacket and an outer shell of waterproof jacket and trousers is a good start. Warm gloves, a hat and gaiters are also useful.

Sleeping bag If you are staying in refuges in the summer months a two-season sleeping bag will suffice. If you plan to bivouac or trek in winter then a three- or four-season bag and a waterproof bivvy bag will be necessary.

Crampons and ice-axe Apart from in the height of the summer, walking crampons and an ice-axe can be not only useful but essential.

Maps and compass Always carry maps covering the complete area of your chosen trek, along with a proper walking compass.

Emergency equipment A brightly coloured two-person emergency bivvy bag should be carried (it also doubles as a rucksack liner).

Sun protection High-factor sunscreen is vital in both summer and winter.

Special equipment Very useful is an altimeter or a GPS (Geographical Positioning System). Proper training in the use of any of this equipment is essential.

Mobile phones Although somewhat controversial, the carrying of a mobile phone could save your life. If you do carry one be aware that you will not always have cover and therefore it cannot be relied upon. Also make sure the batteries are charged and that you do not leave it switched on all day. The emergency services should only be contacted if a situation cannot be resolved by members of your group.

FOOD AND WATER

One of the most essential components of equipment which is frequently disregarded is food. To have too little food or water can be very dangerous as food means energy, which you will need a lot of on a high mountain trek. Manned refuges, where meals can be provided by the refuge staff, are usually only a day's walk of one another. The refuges might also have a small stock of tinned food that can be purchased for lunch the following day. It's a good idea to take a stock of energy bars with you.

During the spring, water is abundant in the mountains. During the summer months, however, finding water might become a real problem, as a lot of the streams and springs dry out. In the summer, at least four litres of water per person should be carried unless you are sure of a source ahead of you. Any water found higher than the highest village is normally drinkable, especially if it is from a spring.

Dehydration can be a serious problem in the summer, and it is recommended that you carry a vitamin preparation to help replace lost minerals and vitamins if dehydration occurs.

WHEN TO TREK

The best and most beautiful time for travelling to the north of Spain is undoubtedly the spring and autumn. While in April the higher mountains are still largely snow-capped, the months of May and June are perhaps the most suitable for trekking. There is a marvellous stillness in the woods and mountains, although the warming sun lures the animals from their winter hiding-places and the flowers are in full bloom.

The summer months of July and August are the most convenient season for high mountain treks, with long hours of daylight and fairly stable weather, although temperatures can

Waterfalls can often provide icy refreshment during a trek on a hot summer's day.

get extremely hot. However, this time of year is also extremely busy as Spain and other European countries tend to take their holidays at the same time. Every year thousands of Spaniards escape to the mountains in search of cool mountain breezes or the refreshing shade of the woods along the brooks and rivers. During these months it is nearly impossible to find a vacant room in hotels or refuges, and the only way to ensure accommodation is to book well in advance.

During September and October the masses have vanished and silence once again returns to the forests and mountains. With the autumn sun lower on the horizon and lucidity in the air, walking through the multicoloured forests of red and orange hues is an unforgettable experience. From the middle of October, at higher altitudes, one should be aware that the first snowfalls will shortly arrive and there will be a chance of frost during the night.

BASIC RULES OF THE NATIONAL PARKS

- It is strictly forbidden to take or damage either plants or minerals of any description.
- It is forbidden to fish, hunt, track or purposely disturb any species of animal.
- It is forbidden to light any fires (unless with camping stoves).
- It is forbidden to leave any rubbish. All rubbish must be brought back with you.
- In the premises of the national park you may neither camp nor bivouac; you may stay only in the refuges provided.
- The circulation of vehicles and bikes is restricted and only allowed by special permission.
- It is forbidden to play either radios or musical instruments or to make any other unnatural noise that may cause alarm to wild animals.
- Dogs should be kept on leads at all times.
- It is forbidden to bathe in or practice any type of watersport on the rivers and lakes.

TREKKING GRADES

Please remember that it is impossible to be absolutely precise about how hard a walk may be, as there may be many contributory factors. The main benefit of grading is to provide you with an overall indicator to compare one walk against another. We have, therefore, looked at the following five factors before deciding the grade:

- Length of trek and length of walking day.
- Average altitude and altitude gain and loss.
- Temperature range and likely weather conditions.
- Trail conditions.
- Remoteness to services and general level of comfort.

A young deer takes shelter in the undergrowth.

Clearly, conditions for a particular trek may vary from one month to the next. The grades we have given are for normal summer conditions, so please take this into account before deciding which trek to attempt.

Easy

Experience is not necessary at this level: anyone who is in good health and fit enough to enjoy a good weekend hill walk can manage this. Usually, 'easy' treks are short in duration and at lower altitudes. However, walking always involves some exertion – trails are seldom flat and you must still expect to have a reasonable amount of ascent and descent. You would normally walk for four to seven hours a day.

Moderate

Most people who enjoy a weekend in the hills or mountains at home are capable of undertaking a trek at this level: you need to be in good health and reasonably fit, and you will almost certainly be taking regular exercise. A trek may be graded 'moderate' if it is a fairly easy medium-duration walk, or if it is a harder, shorter walk. Some walking at higher altitude and the occasional longer or more difficult day may be involved, but generally conditions underfoot will be fair. You would normally walk for five to eight hours a day.

Strenuous

For any trek at this level, fitness is most important and previous trekking experience is highly desirable. Most 'strenuous' treks are equivalent to extended walking in mountainous terrain, but usually at a significantly high altitude. Climate and remoteness can also play a part. You would normally walk for six to eight hours a day, although there may be some longer days.

Tough

At this level, previous experience of trekking is recommended, and you need complete confidence in your physical condition and your ability to trek for many days without a break. You must be able to cope with difficulty underfoot – terrain such as scree, snow or difficult paths on steep mountainsides. Extremes of weather may also be encountered, and on some treks it may be necessary to use an ice-axe and crampons. Stamina is very important, as you may walk from six to nine hours, or even longer, each day.

CLIMBING

In the mid 19th century the mountains of Northern Spain started to attract all sorts of people, not only mountaineers, from near and far. By the early 20th century, geologists, mining engineers, military surveyors and shepherds had claimed the majority of first ascents.

The attention of climbers then shifted to the ascent of more difficult faces. In 1962, the five-day ascent of the West Wall of El Naranjo de Bulnes in the Picos de Europa by Alberto Rabadà and Ernesto Navarro marked a pinnacle of achievement on a route that remains a classic of Spanish climbing.

Until the 1970s these difficult ascents typically involved aid climbing. More recently, the focus for groundbreaking development has shifted to free climbing, often with bolt protection. This has resulted in physically and technically demanding routes on lower lying cliffs and crags which provide variety and contrast to the earlier mountain ascents. As a consequence, today Northern Spain has much to offer climbers of all abilities and persuasions.

CLIMBING GRADES

The peaks that require a scramble to the summit are graded thus:

The monolithic Naranjo de Bulnes provide a fantastic backdrop on several of the routes in the Picos de Europa (chapter 7).

Grade 1 – Straightforward for experienced walkers. Only occasional use of hands necessary. Exposure is minimal.

Grade 2 – Hands required for more sustained sections, exposure may be significant, and you may wish to carry a rope for any particularly exposed sections.

Grade 3 – Moves on steep rock in very exposed situations. Rope protection will be required on occasion unless you are very experienced. Some routes at this grade are recognized rock climbs.

If more than a scramble, the peaks are graded according to the alpine grading system:
F (*facile*) – Snow climbs, with slopes up to 40°, and maybe some very easy rock scrambling.
PD (*peu difficile*) – Slightly steeper snow slopes, and longer, more sustained sections of scrambling.
AD (*assez difficile*) – Can involve some pitched climbing on rock, snow or ice.

MAPS

Topographical maps of Spain are issued by two government agencies: the IGN (Instituto Geográfico Nacional) and the SGE (Servicio Geográfico del Ejército), although in the northern alpine areas maps produced by Editorial Alpina are more practical.

SPANISH WALKING ORGANIZATIONS

Federación Española de Montañismo (FEM)
Tel.: 91-445-13-82
Umbrella organization representing walking and climbing and walkers' and climbers' interests.

Federación Española de Deportes de Montaña (FEDME)
C/Alberto Aguilera 3-4, 28015 Madrid
Similar organization to the above.

4

EASTERN (CATALUNIAN) PYRENEES

FRANCE
Toulouse
Andorra la Vella
Bilbao
ANDORRA
Barcelona
SPAIN
PORTUGAL
Madrid
Palma
Lisbon

Whether your interests lie in geology, geography, history, natural history, or just plain old scenic beauty, the Eastern Pyrenees will not fail to satisfy.

Huge glacial lakes, remnants of an industrial past and ancient monasteries, rare plant species and wild deer, soaring peaks outlined against sun-drenched valleys are only a few of the elements to be encountered on tramps through this region.

Superlative sunrises are best experienced in the month of September, when both the days and the nights are clear and bright, as seen here at Estany Negre (trek 3).

The Catalunian Pyrenees – defined for the purpose of this book as the region between the Vall de Camprodón and the Parque Nacional d'Aigüestortes Estany de Sant Maurici – may not be as high as their western counterparts, but they are every bit as spectacular. Lush, green valleys nestled among snow-capped peaks are home to hundreds of isolated communities, many of which still retain their own dialects and languages. Here, too, is the historically fascinating Principality of Andorra, as well as the Parque Nacional d'Aigüestortes Estany de Sant Maurici, one of only two national parks in the Pyrenees and one of only 10 in all of Spain.

One of the Catalunian Pyrenees' greatest attractions is surely its towns and villages, with their stone and slate-roofed homes and elegant, medieval churches. Many of these communities originally grew up to accommodate the *trashumancia* – the annual migration of shepherds, cowherds and their charges from the plains to the more fertile Pyrenean meadows – or developed around monasteries. The town of Ripoll, for instance, was founded in 888 when the first count of Barcelona, the wonderfully named Guifré el Pilós, or Wilfred

the Hairy, established a Benedictine monastery there. The town, which went on to become a hub of medieval religious thought, is still home to the monastery's 12th-century church of Santa Maria. The church boasts a magnificent Romanesque portico, which depicts the glory of God and creation through elaborately sculpted friezes.

La Seu d'Urgell

La Seu d'Urgell, the biggest town in the Catalunian Pyrenees, is similarly dominated by a church. The 12th-century cathedral of Santa Maria, seat of the regional archbishopric since the 6th century and famous for its multicoloured rose window and 13th-century cloister with 50 exquisitely carved columns, is easily the most beautiful cathedral in the Pyrenees. The cathedral towers over the city's medieval centre, which has beautiful arcaded streets and overhanging galleries.

Principality of Andorra

La Seu d'Urgell's history is inextricably tied up with that of its unusual northern neighbour, the Principality of Andorra. According to legend, the emperor Charlemagne founded Andorra in the 8th century out of gratitude to the locals, who led his troops through the mountains on their way to the Spanish peninsula to challenge the Arab occupants. Charlemagne's grandson later bequeathed Andorra to the count of La Seu d'Urgell, who in turn passed it along to the town's bishop. Following an altercation in the 13th century, leadership of Andorra was divided between the bishop of La Seu d'Urgell and the counts of Foix, a title that has since been yielded to the French president. To this day, France and Spain share suzerainty over this mini-state, which possesses a number of small, beautifully preserved villages.

Val d'Aran – the Aran Valley

Like Andorra, the character of the Val d'Aran, the Pyrenees' only Atlantic valley, reflects a mixed French and Spanish influence. Originally part of Aquitanian Comminges, the Val d'Aran only joined Catalunia in the 14th century. The result is a culture that is politically Spanish-leaning, but French in practically every other respect. The valley's architec-

Barns are usually constructed from locally sourced materials. In this case, a wooden doorpost is fixed into stone brackets top and bottom to allow the door to open easily.

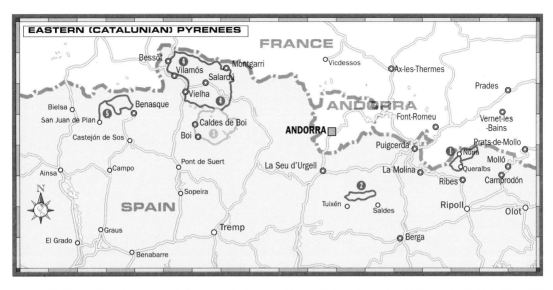

ture, with its conical towers and dormer windows, is decidedly French, as is Aranés, the local language, a dialect of Gascon French that is still spoken by many of the valley's 6,200 inhabitants.

Parque Nacional d'Aigüestortes Estany de Sant Maurici

Just to the south of the Val d'Aran is the Parque Nacional d'Aigüestortes, which contains some of the mountain range's most stunning scenery.

Unspoilt forests and meadows, and more than 50 lakes and tarns – most notably the Estany de Sant Maurici – nestle between the twin peaks of Los Encantats. The region was declared a national park by General Franco himself. As the general passed through the area on other business, he was so taken by its natural beauty that he ordered the immediate creation of a national park. The Parque Nacional d'Aigüestortes Estany de Sant Maurici was duly inaugurated in 1955.

The terrain of the Valle de Gistain in the Catalunian Pyrenees can be exhausting and inhospitable at times (trek 5).

TREK 1: THROUGH THE VALLE DE NÚRIA

At a distance of about 100km (60 miles) from the Mediterranean lies the Puigmal massif. This massif, the first on the eastern side of the Pyrenees, rises to approximately 3000m (9850ft) above sea level. This area, being one of the oldest sections of the Pyrenees, has a long and lively geological history. The impressive, sharp rock formations of the Río del Freser and Río Núria gorges consist mainly of crystalline rock, while the final shape of the landscape was carved out by the glaciers that once covered all of the valleys and reached down as far as Queralbs.

TREK ESSENTIALS

LENGTH: 3 days; 47.25km (28¾ miles).
ACCESS: From Figueras or Girona take the N260 or C150 to Olot and continue to Ripoll; turn right onto the C152 to Ribes de Freser; in the middle of the village turn right and on to Queralbs. From Barcelona, take the N152 north and drive to Ripoll and then as above. From Llerida, take the C1313 to La Seu; from here follow the N260 to Belver and then on the N152 via La Molina to Ribes de Freser and Queralbs.
DIFFICULTY: Moderate, with one long descent of 1700m.
HIGHEST POINT: Puigmal 2910m (9547ft).
TREK STYLE: Refuges.
MAPS: Editorial Alpina 1:25 000 Puigmal Valle de Núria.
FURTHER OPTIONS: From Núria it is possible to go directly to Collada de Fontalba, thus avoiding the ascent of Puigmal.

During the summer months the alpine pastures above the tree-line have been used as grazing for cattle, sheep and horses for centuries. With the recent decline in agriculture, many of the round, stone shepherds' huts that are dotted across the countryside have fallen into disrepair. Long important to the economy of these densely wooded valleys are hunting and fishing, and today much of the area is a National Hunting Reserve.

Queralbs to Refugio de Coma de Vaca
The starting point is the romantically situated mountain village of Queralbs, above the Río del Freser. At the entrance to the village (opposite the car-park), is a well-marked and almost impossible-to-miss sign marking the GR11 (red/white way-marks) path to Núria, a former cloister that has been converted into a luxury hotel. A steep slope leads past the last houses in the village. This broad pilgrims' path, which has been partly sur-faced through arduous work with natural stone, at first follows alongside the railway line.

After about 45 minutes you reach the start of the Valle de Núria. A vertiginous but good path is cut into the mountainside. After about 1½ hours a small bridge is reached – cross the river and

CLIMATE OF THE VALLE DE NÚRIA AND PUIGMAL MASSIF

This area is located relatively close to the Mediterranean and, as such, is subject to special climatic conditions. The highest precipitation levels occur in August, when heavy thunderstorms build up near the Ebro valley and get trapped in the mountain ranges that rise from the coast. When the heavens open, these thunderstorms should not be underestimated.

The low-lying valleys, up to approximately 1000m (3280ft), are noted for their typical Mediterranean climate; while above, a harsh alpine environment rules, with its characteristic animal and plant life.

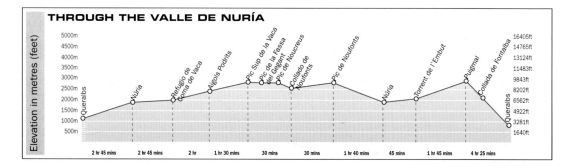

THROUGH THE VALLE DE NURÍA

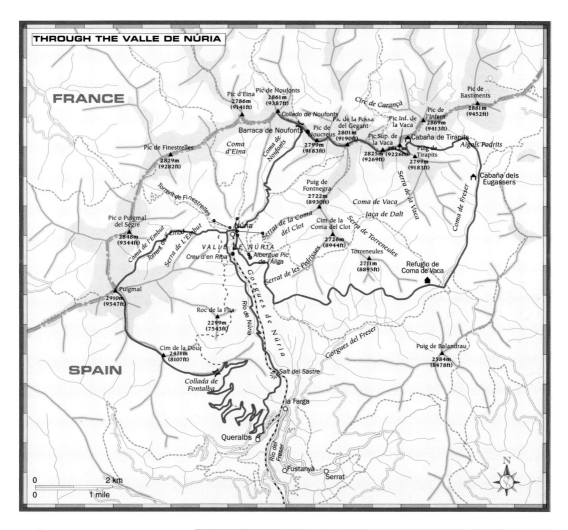

THROUGH THE VALLE DE NÚRIA

continue in zigzags up a steep slope. Breathtaking views back along the gorge show the railway line clinging to the cliffs. The route becomes more gentle and, after crossing the rounded summit of a glacial moraine with the Creu d'en Riba cross on the top, an amazing panorama is revealed. Situated in the middle of the valley ahead, Núria is reached after about 2¾–3 hours' walking from Queralbs. Those who want to avoid the first exhausting

From Collada de Fontalba it is possible to see right into the Valle de Núria; Pic de Noufonts stands out in the background.

The wooded gorge of the Río del Freser cuts deep into the surrounding countryside.

800m (2625ft) of the steep but beautiful ascent can reach Núria by train on the rack and pinion railway (see page 36).

From the railway station in Núria head south towards the Albergue Pic de l'Àliga. Continuing south above the Gorgues de Núria (Núria Gorge), you will have fantastic views of the Catalunian plains. After about 30 minutes, cross a small saddle and follow the path which turns abruptly to the left and eastwards into the Gorgues del Freser (Río del Freser Gorge), which is characterized by jagged, rocky outcrops. The well-distinguished trail passes an old, round shepherd's hut. As evening approaches and silence falls on the mountains it isn't uncommon to see chamoix grazing among the alpine pastures. After approximately 5–6 hours of walking you will eventually reach the manned Refugio de Coma de Vaca (1995m/6545ft).

Refugio de Coma de Vaca to Núria

The path heads north from the refuge into the wide Coma de Freser valley. After passing the Cabaña dels Eugassers, turn off to the left and continue once more on the GR11, which is followed westwards towards the Pics de la Vaca ahead. Only a few metres below the summit another *cabaña* (hut) is reached at 2700m (8858ft) above sea level. Continue west along the ridge to reach the Pic de La Fossa del Gegant (2801m/9190ft) after about 4 hours of walking.

Staying on the ridge, the Pic de Noucreus (2799m/9183ft) is passed before reaching the pass of Collado de Noufonts (2727m/8947ft). Finally the barren and stony summit of the Pic de Noufonts at 2861m (9386ft) is reached. After enjoying the marvellous views from the top backtrack to Collado de Noufonts and head south-west on the GR11 into the valley of Coma de Noufonts and on to Núria (1960m/6430ft).

The night can be spent either in luxury in the hotel, or in more basic accommodation at the refuge or on the campsite behind the hotel.

Núria to Queralbs

From Núria it is possible to climb the highest peak in the area, Puigmal (2910m/9547ft). Leave Núria heading west and cross the bridge over the Torrent de Finestrelles and trek into an area of black pine trees. After gaining open ground, the Torrent de l'Embut is quickly encountered. Cross the stream and climb up the steep Coma de l'Embut, following the course of the stream; please note that the stream can often run dry in the summer months. On leaving the stream behind, climb the stony north-eastern side of Puigmal. From the summit, with its iron cross, there are overwhelming panoramas towards the west, with a large portion of the eastern Pyrenees visible as far as Andorra. Looking eastwards on a clear day the view stretches to the Mediterranean coast.

Descend the path on the south-south-westerly flank of the mountain, following it to the start of the jeep track at Collada de Fontalba (2100m/6890ft). From the col there are marvellous views back towards Núria and a large part of the trek. Follow the zigzagging track for the remaining 1000m (3280ft) of descent back to Queralbs (1100m/3609ft).

Puigmal, as seen from the Collada de Fontalba, is an easy ascent for summit-baggers.

NÚRIA MONASTERY

At the foot of the Puigmal massif, 2000m (6560ft) above sea level, lies the once influential and powerful Núria monastery, which gives its name to the valley. The monastery was first documented by Pope Alexander in the 12th century but, due to the increase in secularism and the monastery's location in a picturesque alpine landscape, it has since been converted into the luxurious Valle de Núria Hotel.

The scenery surrounding the cloister is impressive, with the looming Puigmal peak nearby; also visible are Pic de Segre, Pic de Eina, Pic de Noufonts and the Pic Fossa del Gegant. The former cloister and its effigy of the Virgin, Mare de Déu de Núria, is one of the region's most popular tourist features, and is accessed via the rack and pinion railway from Ribes.

THE RACK AND PINION RAILWAY

For centuries, the Núria cloister lay forlorn and remote, reachable only on foot through the deep and isolated Núria Gorge. At over 2000 metres (6560 feet) above sea level, access to both visitors and pilgrims alike was not only difficult but also dangerous. In 1916 the cloister was opened to the public in winter for the first time, which generated a need for either road or railway access.

It was no surprise that once the technological revolution started and the subsequent advancement in engineering techniques that plans were made to improve access to the cloister. Intensive meetings were held in 1917 about the pros and cons of either a road or a train connection. The Bishop D'Urgell, Joan Benolloch was an eager advocate of the project, with the aim of increasing the number of visitors to the cloister. However, due to the enormous technical difficulties involved, plans were quickly dropped.

In 1924 the Empresa Ferrocarriles de Montaña de Grandes Pendientes (FMGP) carried out a detailed feasibility study into the prospect of a rack and pinion railway. Eventually, after nine years of planning, on 20 November 1926, the Spanish government finally gave the green light for construction – the project was duly started on 24 May 1928.

For the construction of the railway embankment, consisting of numerous tunnels and bridges which gain over 1000m (3280ft) in height and later, the laying of the track itself, over 800 men were employed. Work was started in both Ribes and in Núria. The tracks, which cover 12.5km (7½ miles), were finally installed at the beginning of 1930, and relieved the problem of transporting the workers and materials while also serving to test this incredible structure. Then, on 30 September 1930, a steam engine travelled the complete distance between Ribes and Núria for the first time. On 22 March 1931, the Cremallera (Zipper) railway was finally opened to the general public.

Today, the steam engines have been retired and modern diesel/electric locomotives, which cover the distance in 45 minutes at an average speed of 19kph, work throughout the summer. In the winter months, the line continues to operate while the ski resort is open, and in the event of a heavy snowfall a snow plough capable of removing 800 tons of snow per hour is employed to clear the track.

The railway track starts in the small town of Ribes, but also stops in the village of Ribes Vila, where the main station and maintenance shed are located. From here, it journeys on to Rialb and, shortly after, the ascent starts in earnest. After passing through Queralbs it enters the Fontalba tunnel before finally reaching its destination at Núria, 1964m (6444ft) above sea level.

The rack and pinion railway cuts an impressive route therough the Núria Gorge.

FLORA AND FAUNA OF THE PUIGMAL MASSIF AND THE VALLE DE NÚRIA

The lower mountain-sides of the Puigmal massif are dominated by extensive black pine forests (*Pinus nigra*), which end abruptly at about 2000m (6500ft). Alongside the riverbanks and brooks you will still find some uncultivated woods, comprising of alders (*Alnus glutinosa*), different types of willow (*Salix*), rowan (*Sorbus aucuparia*) and the widespread hazel (*Corylus avllana*). Where the robust black pine is absent, the rowan can frequently be found growing alongside beech (*Fagus sylvatica*) and oak (*Quercus*) to form stunning mixed deciduous forests. Alpine rose (*Rosa pendulina*) and sloes (*Prunus spinosa*) blossom in the sub-growth and clearings.

These woodlands are also inhabited by several little nocturnal creatures, such as the Garden dormouse (*Eliomys quercinus*) and the Edible (Fat) dormouse (*Glis glis*). Their preference for the dark makes them very difficult to spot, particularly the Fat dormouse which has a reputation for hibernating for up to nine months of the year.

As height is gained to the alpine level many interesting plants and flowers can be found. Here prosper a multitude of different gentians (*Gentiana*), fringed pinks (*Dianthus superbus*), Alpine pasque flowers (*Pusatilla alpina*) and the Poet's narcissus (*Narcissus poeticus*), to mention only a few.

The most common of mammals is surely the agile chamois (*Rupicapra rupicapra*), which can often be seen. Also to be found are mouflon (*Ovis orientalis*), with their marvellous horns, and marmots (*Marmota marmota*) – this amusing little creature, with its unmistakable warning cry, is well worth the patience to watch. As one sits down quietly on a rock, the marmot believes that the danger has passed and it will come out of its burrow and start, under the watchful eyes of its neighbours, to search for food eagerly. The red fox (*Vulpes vulpes*) can also be found along with different species of pine marten (*Martes martes*).

Bonelli's eagles (*Hieraaetus fasciatus*) and golden eagles (*Aquila chrysaetos*) rule the skies, while a variety of dippers (*Cinclus cinclus*) dart along the rivers and brooks.

The hardy Alpine gentian (*Gentiana nivalis*) has firmly set its roots into this often inclement alpine pasture.

During the winter, chamoix often gather in large groups with their young from the previous summer.

TREK 2: SIERRA DEL CADÍ AND PEDRAFORCA

South of Andorra and away from the main Pyrenean range lies a small but extremely abrupt range of mountains called the Sierra del Cadí. It extends from east to west over 20km (12 miles) and at its highest elevation, the Puig de La Canal Baridana, it attains a height of 2647m (8684ft). Because of its special ecological interest an extensive area of this mainly limestone massif became a special conservation area – the Natural Park of Cadí–Moixeró – in 1983.

TREK ESSENTIALS

LENGTH: 3 days; 46.75km (28 miles).
ACCESS: From Barcelona take the A18 motorway north, and leave at junction 17 to take the C1411. After approximately 60km (37½ miles), at Berga, take the B400 to Gòsol and on to Josa de Cadí.
DIFFICULTY: Moderate, although if an ascent is going to be made of Pedraforca care should be exercised as some easy scrambling is required.
HIGHEST POINT: Puig de la Canal Baridana 2647m (8684ft).
TREK STYLE: Refuges.
MAPS: Editorial Alpina Sierra del Cadí/Gòsol.
FURTHER OPTIONS: Ascent of Pedraforca.

More than 25 million years ago a gigantic inland sea once existed in this region, which over a period of time left a limestone deposit several hundred metres thick. Later, the land was forced upwards and erosion of the limestone by the weather began. The karst landscape that was left behind and its accompanying flora and fauna make the Sierra del Cadí stand out from the neighbouring countryside.

Josa de Cadí to Refugio Prat d'Aguiló

The starting point of this walk is the small, picturesque mountain hamlet of Josa de Cadí (1430m/4692ft). Dominated by a church high up on a rocky outcrop overlooking the houses, Josa de

Cadí is best reached from Tuixèn or Gòsol along a newly constructed road. From the far side of the hamlet take the north-westerly path signposted for the 12th-century chapel. Follow the path alongside the Torrent de Juvell, which is frequently dried up during the summer months. After about 1 hour the Coll de Jovell is reached with nice views all around. Take the path that heads west-north-west and contours across the southern slopes of the Sierra del Cadí. After approximately another hour, at the Coll de Pi del'Orri, take a sharp right turning to the north-west and climb a karst slope strewn with isolated pines. A steep climb up a zigzagging path leads to the Porto del Cadí (2500m/8202ft).

Follow the ridge eastwards over the top of Torre de Cadí (2567m/8422ft), the twin peaks of Pics de les Tres Canaletes (2612m/8570ft and 2618m/8589ft) and finally onto the highest in the range, Puig de la Canal Baridana (2647m/8684ft). Before continuing, take time to enjoy the panorama. The route now heads along the ridge and takes in a few more peaks before reaching the Coll de Prat d'Aguiló at 2410m (7874ft). Descend northwards from the col and the manned Refugio Prat d'Aguiló (2031m/6663ft) is reached after a descent of some 400m (1312ft).

Refugio Prat d'Aguiló to Refugio Lluis Estasen

This day's walk is a little shorter than yesterday, so there is plenty of time to enjoy more breathtaking views of the Sierra del Cadí. Leave the refuge and return back up to the Coll de Prat d'Aguiló.

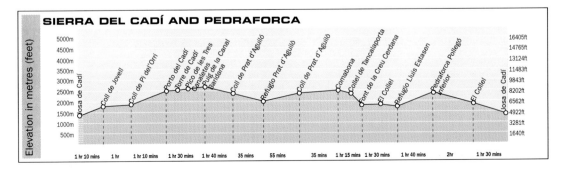

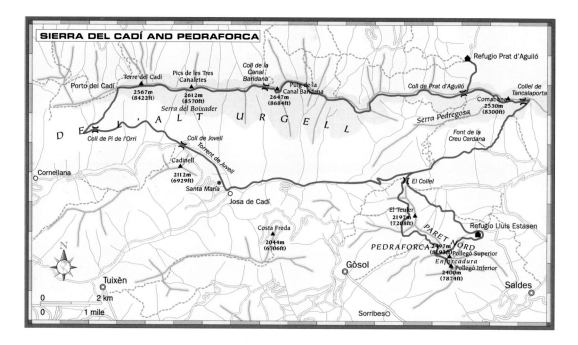

Turn left towards the east to eventually reach the barren, rounded hilltop of the Comabona (2530m/8300ft). Go over the summit and down the other side until you reach the Collel de Tancalaporta (2400m/7874ft), where the path descends to the right in a south-westerly direction. Follow the path through a forest full of old, twisted pine trees and then downwards across scrubland until you reach a forestry track and a spring, Font de La Creu Cerdana (1850m/6070ft). Turn right into the forest, heading west to El Collell pass (1845m/6053ft) where there are marvellous views of the twin-peaked Pedraforca standing high above the valley of Saldes. 'Pedraforca' means 'stone fork,' and it is a fork that is now the symbol of the park.

The track now heads south-east and is easily followed to the manned Refugio Lluis Estasen

Pedraforca rises behind the south flanks of the Sierra del Cadí.

The south face of the dominant Pedraforca mountain clearly shows its two twin peaks – Pollegó Superior and Pollegó Inferior.

FLORA AND FAUNA OF THE NATIONAL PARK OF CADÍ-MOIXERÓ

The National Park of Cadí-Moixero has three distinct altitudes and, therefore, varying climatic conditions that result in a wide variety of plant life. The high alpine slopes above 2000m (6560ft) are covered with a great diversity of colourful flowers, such as gentians (*Gentiana*), carline thistle (*Carlina vulgaris*), saffron (*Safra bord*) and the alpine rose (*Pulsatilla*) (thistle pictured).

Lower down at subalpine level, and well-adapted to withstand the extreme climatic conditions, black pine (*Pinus nigra*) proliferate on the mountain-side, while on the forest floor Dwarf junipers (*Juniperus nana*), and rhododendron (*Rhododendron ferrugineum*) blossom. On the lower north-facing slopes of the hills are firs (*Abies alba*), while on the southern side the shaded areas are populated by beech (*Fagus sylvatica*), while the sunny spots are occupied by oak trees (*Quercus pubescens*). These deciduous forests are also interspersed with Scots pine (*Pinus sylvestris*).

It's also possible to observe the rare bearded vulture (*Gypaëtus barbatus*) and the more common griffon vulture (*Gyps fulvus*). In addition to the golden eagle (*Aquila chrysaetos*), the short-toed eagle (*Ciraetus gallicus*), which is characteristic of Mediterranean karst areas, along with Bonelli's eagle (*Hieraaetus fasciatus*) are also found here. The gems of this beautiful sierra, however, must surely be the Tengmalm's owl (*Aegolius funereus*), the capercaillie (*Tetrao urogallus*) and the black woodpecker (*Dryocopus martius*), all three of which are very rare in Spain.

The picturesque village of Gòsol was once home to the surrealist artist Salvador Dali (1904–89).

(1700m/5577ft). From the refuge's privileged location at the foot of Pedraforca one is once again rewarded with marvellous views of the Saldes valley and the surrounding mountains.

Refugio Lluis Estasen to Josa de Cadí

Today there is the chance to climb one or both of the twin peaks of Pedraforca. Leave the refuge and head west, following the path that goes across the forested west slopes of Pedraforca at an altitude of about 1800m (5900ft). After about 45 minutes follow a long steep scree slope south to the l'Enfocadura saddle, which separates the two peaks. The upper peak, Pollegó Superior, is the most accessible, and can be reached by climbing the craggy path from the saddle. Care should be taken as a small amount of scrambling is required.

Return down the same route to the saddle, and descend the west slope of Pedraforca following the path that heads north-west. You will soon enter a dense pine forest, and after walking for about 1–1½ hours cross a little stream to a junction about 200m (180yd) beyond. At the junction take the path to the north, just below a ridge. After about 20 minutes the jeep track at El Collell col is rejoined. Take the turning on the left and follow the track all the way back down the valley to Josa de Cadí.

TREK 3: A THOUSAND AND ONE LAKES

As dusk approaches and the sky turns red over this theatre of Spanish mountains, the observer will witness the dark silhouette of the surrounding towers mirrored in the still waters of plentiful lakes. A journey through this central region of the D'Aigüestortes Estany de Sant Maurici National Park takes you through areas of exceptional natural beauty. Beneath the soaring peaks, icy-cold cascading waterfalls feed numerous glacial lakes. On leaving the low-level pine forests a rocky landscape awaits, where timid chamoix and deer will greet the traveller, while skywards eagles and vultures roam the thermals.

TREK ESSENTIALS

LENGTH: 6 days.

ACCESS: From Lérida take the N230 to Barbastro, then to Benabarre and finally to Boi.

DIFFICULTY: Easy to moderate. There is no more than 500-600m (1640-2000ft) of ascent per day.

HIGHEST POINT: Collada de Saburó 2689m (8822ft).

TREK STYLE: Refuges (hotel in Boi).

MAPS: Mapa Excursionista y Turistico 1:25 000 Sant Maurici.

FURTHER OPTIONS: An easier option on the last day is to walk to Refugio d'Éstany Llong instead of Boi, saving some 4 hours of walking. From the refuge you can then follow the 11-km (6½-mile) jeep track to the pretty San Nicolau valley and then walk a further 2km (1¼ miles) to Boi; or just hire a 4x4 from the Refugio d'Éstany Llong.

RESTRICTIONS: No wild camping, open fires or fishing.

Boi to Refugio Ventosa i Galvell

From the little mountain village of Boi take a taxi to the Cavallers dam (the taxi stand is by the church in the village square). The walk starts at a height of 1781m (5840ft) amid a high mountain landscape.

From the car-park follow the track to the top of the dam and then take the wide path that goes along the lakeside. After about half an hour you reach the end of the reservoir. From here follow wooden posts with yellow markings on the right-hand side of the river to a small bridge, where you cross the Riuet del Negre. Ascend a zigzagging path, surrounded by waterfalls. Some 2 hours later you will reach the lake of Estany Negre (2127m/6978ft). Follow the path round the north side of the lake until you reach Refugio Ventosa i Galvell (2225m/7300ft).

After an excellent dinner in the hut you can enjoy a vivid sunset behind the 3000-m (9850-ft) Besiberri mountain range.

Refugio Ventosa i Galvell to Refugio de Colomèrs

From just behind the refuge follow a narrow path downhill in a south-westerly direction to the Estany Negre. Head east following a river past three small lakes. From the last lake, Estany de Colieto, head east and climb up a scree slope to another lake, Estany Tort. Continue up the Tallada Llarga valley to the Pòrt de Colomèrs pass (2600m/8530ft) where you will be rewarded with stunning views of the Val d'Aran to the north; to the south is the entire D'Aigüestortes Estany de Sant Maurici National Park with its many impressive peaks.

The trek continues down into the striking glacial valley of Terme de Naut d'Aran, which is full of lakes. Follow the valley on the right-hand side of the river and continue downhill to the lake of Estanh Major de Colomèrs (2120m/6955ft). The Refugio de Colomèrs can be found just above the dam.

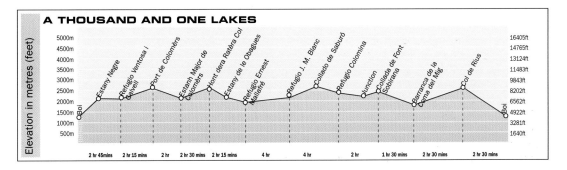

A THOUSAND AND ONE LAKES

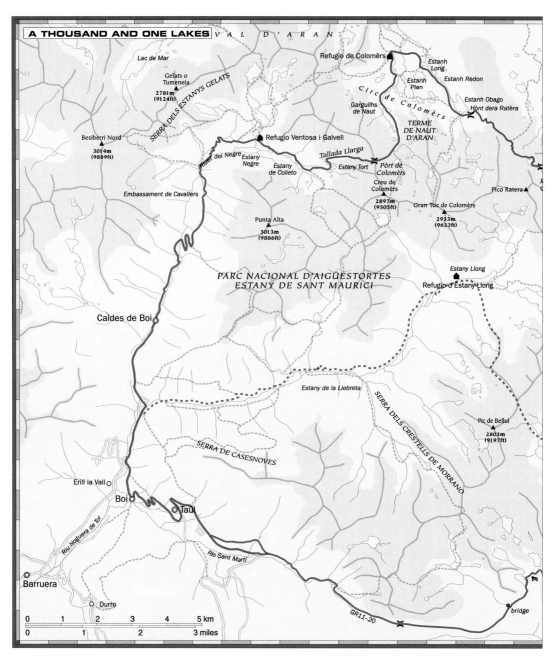

A THOUSAND AND ONE LAKES VAL D'ARAN

Lac de Mar

Gelats o Tumenela

2781m (9124ft)

SERRA DELS ESTANYS GELATS

Refugio de Colomèrs

Estanh Long

Estanh Plan

Estanh Redon

Circ de Colomèrs

Garguilhs de Naut

Estanh Obago

Hònt dera Ratèra

Besiberri Nord

3014m (9889ft)

Refugio Ventosa i Galvell

TERME DE NAUT D'ARAN

Riuet del Negre

Estany Negre

Tallada Llarga

Estany de Colieto

Estany Tort

Pòrt de Colomèrs

Embassament de Cavallers

Creu de Colomèrs

2897m (9505ft)

Gran Tuc de Colomèrs

Pico Ratera

Punta Alta

3013m (9886ft)

2933m (9623ft)

PARC NACIONAL D'AIGÜESTORTES
ESTANY DE SANT MAURICI

Estany Llong

Refugio d'Estany Llong

Caldes de Boi

Estany de la Liebreta

SERRA DELS CRESTELLS DE MORRANO

Pic de Bellui

2803m (9197ft)

SERRA DE CASESNOVES

Erill-la Vall

Boi

Taul

Riu Noguera de Tor

Rio Sant Marti

Barruera

Durro

GR11-20

bridge

| 0 | 1 | 2 | 3 | 4 | 5 km |
| 0 | | 1 | | 2 | 3 miles |

Refugio de Colomèrs to Refugio Ernest Mallafrè

Cross the lake's dam and join the GR11, which is marked with red and white paint. Ascend slightly for a short distance until the path levels off and heads in a south-easterly direction. The path now continues past another three lakes: Estanh Long, Estanh Redon and Estanh Obago (2200m/ 7217ft). From the lakes follow a zigzagging path uphill until you reach the Hònt dera Ratèra pass (2500m/8202ft). Looking back, there are great

views of pine forests, lakes and mountains. Continue on and be sure not to take any of the junctions to the left or right.

On re-entering the national park follow the GR11 path marked with yellow posts for 200m (180yd) downhill, heading right and to the north of Estany de Ratèra. Go downhill through a pine forest where there is a possibility of seeing chamoix and deer. Follow the path to the left of lake Estany de les Obagues de Ratèra (2230m/

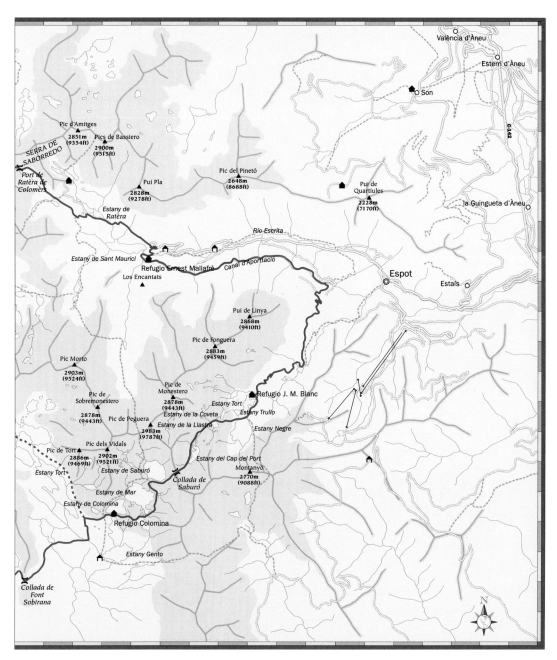

València d'Àneu
Esterri d'Àneu
Son
C-142
Pic d'Amitges
2851m
(9354ft)
Pics de Bassiero
2900m
(9515ft)
SERRA DE SABORREDO
Port de Ratèra de Colomèrs
Pui Pla
2828m
(9278ft)
Pic del Pinetó
2648m
(8688ft)
Pui de Quartiules
2228m
(7170ft)
la Guingueta d'Àneu
Estany de Ratèra
Río Escrita
Estany de Sant Maurici
Refugio Ernest Mallafrè
Canal d'Aportació
Los Encantats
Espot
Estaís
Pui de Linya
2868m
(9410ft)
Pic de Fonguera
2883m
(9459ft)
Pic Morto
2903m
(9524ft)
Pic de Monestero
2878m
(9443ft)
Refugio J. M. Blanc
Pic de Sobremonestero
Estany Tort
2878m
(9443ft)
Pic de Peguera
Estany de la Coveta
Estany Trullo
Estany de la Llastra
2983m
(9787ft)
Estany Negre
Pic de Tort
Pic dels Vidals
2886m
(9469ft)
2902m
(9521ft)
Estany de Saburó
Estany del Cap del Port
Estany Tort
Estany de Mar
Collada de Saburó
Montanyó
2770m
(9088ft)
Estany de Colomina
Refugio Colomina
Estany Gento
Collada de Font Sobirana
N

7316ft) and then take the path alongside a stream to a wooden bridge. Cross the bridge to join a jeep track. Turn left and, after about 1.5km (1 mile), cross another bridge.

Soon after, a signpost points to the right indicating some *cascadas* (waterfalls). Take the footpath down past the pretty waterfalls and then on to lake Estany de Sant Maurici. Walk round the lake in a clockwise direction to Refugio Ernest Mallafrè (1900m/6234ft). From the hut there are superb

views of the bizarrely shaped, twin-peaked Los Encantats jutting up from the surrounding forest.

Refugio Ernest Mallafrè to Refugio J. M. Blanc

Follow the small path that leads in an easterly direction from behind the refuge. Cross a small stream and after about 200m (180yd) turn left onto a canal path. This canal channels water for a hydroelectricity plant at Espot. Follow the path for about 11km (6½ miles) – on two occasions you will

The view of the beautiful glacial lake of Éstany Negre is particularly good from Refugio Ventosa i Galvell.

of Estany Trullo, where you are rewarded with a 180-degree views of 20 or so peaks that stand above 2800m (9186ft), including Peguera, Monestero and Fonguera.

Refugio J. M. Blanc to Refugio Colomina

Today is an easy day following the GR11-20. From the refuge set off in a southerly direction on a jeep track until you reach the idyllic lake of Estany Negre (although not the same one encountered on the first day of this trek). From here, turn right and cross two small dams. Leaving the lake behind, ascend a small hill to a saddle and continue on to Estany de la Coveta and Estany de la Llastra.

The path goes between these two lakes, and just beyond you will see an old metal signpost to Collada de Saburó. Turn left at the signpost, and follow a stream up the hill and across some scree slopes to pass the inviting crystal-clear waters of Estany del Cap del Port. Continue round the lake and then take the zigzagging path to Collada de Saburó (2689m/8822ft). From the pass descend steeply over loose scree to arrive at Estany de Saburó. Follow the edge of the lake, and after crossing the dam a path heads off to lakes Mar and Colomina; Refugio Colomina (2408m/7900ft) is located on the south side of Estany de Colomina. Looking south from the refuge you will see the gentle lowlands of the Pyrenees.

Refugio Colomina to Boi

Good staying power is required for this long, final day as there are lots of ups and downs. Leave the hut heading west until you reach a junction. Turn left downhill until you reach another junction after 1km (⅔ mile). Turn left again downhill in the direc-

have to bypass some collapsed tunnels by traversing below the canal, rejoining it after a hundred metres or so – until you reach a signpost at a junction: 'Refugio J M Blanc 2 horas'.

Turn right at the signpost and follow the track uphill, initially to a small pass, then through a short tunnel and on to Refugio J. M. Blanc (2300m/8759ft). In the summer months you will have the opportunity to see rare butterflies, such as the apollo and swallowtail. The last kilometre as you approach the refuge is through pine forest. The refuge stands on a spit of land on the banks

D'AIGÜESTORTES ESTANY DE SANT MAURICI NATIONAL PARK

Due to its remote location, the Val d'Aran and the D'Aigüestortes Estany de Sant Maurici National Park have been isolated from the rest of Spain since time immemorial. Only a few shepherds and the occasional hunter dared to go into these unapproachable mountains. Thanks to these centuries of seclusion, the region's culture and customs have changed little up to the present day.

The name 'Aran' is a Basque word and means 'closed' or 'hidden', as this valley was inaccessible from the south and the rest of Spain, penetrable only via the upper reaches of the Río Garona near the French border. The

One of the numerous glacial lakes in the Circ de Colomérs.

valley was first inhabited by the Basque people and had a colourful history in the later Middle Ages until the area, whose residents were then known as 'Araneser', became a protectorate of the Spanish Kingdom in the 11th century. It was not until 1924 however, that the valley finally became part of Spanish territory.

In recent years, the region's agriculture has changed from being mainly subsistence farming to the large-scale production of dairy products for export to the rest of the peninsula. Latterly, tourism has become one of the main sources of income, and Baquèira Beret is one of the biggest ski resorts in the Pyrenees.

The national park, which was founded in 1955, covers about 10,230 hectares, and geologically speaking is one of the oldest parts of the Pyrenees. If all of the peaks of the Pyrenees were characterized by their glacial activity, those of the D'Aigüestortes Estany de Sant Maurici National Park would stand out like no other. The imposing peaks reach heights of over 2800m (9200ft). Towering above what was once a thick ice field, they have been exposed to the effects of the weathering process and bizarre rock formations, like those of Los Encantats, have become a symbol of the park.

More than 50 lakes and lagoons are evidence of this glacial activity. 'Aigüestortes' translates as 'wild water', and the name dates from the time when numerous rivers and creeks ran their natural courses, untouched by man. Today, a network of pipes and dams connects many of the lakes, creating a powerful source of hydroelectricity.

Estany Negre encircled by mountains, as seen from near the Refugio J. M. Blanc.

tion of the upper cable car station, which should be visible in front of you. When you reach another junction at 2200m (7218ft), turn sharp right back on yourself and cross a small river. All along this section there are red dashes of paint on the rocks.

From the river ascend an old paved path which, after 4km (2⅓ miles), leads you to the Collada de Font Sobirana (2441m/8808ft). Descend a steep

zigzagging path and continue along the path until just before the dam of a small lake; turn to the left and you will see a large rock in the middle of a field. Go to the rock and directly behind it you will pick up the path once again. Pass some ruined buildings and mine workings and continue along a miner's path until you reach the Barranca de la Coma del Mig (1800m/5905ft) where there is a collapsed bridge. Cross the river on stepping-stones. On the other side of the river continue uphill over grassy terrain to the Col de Rus pass (2600m/8530ft). From the pass, follow a well-marked path downhill by the side of the Río San Marti until you reach a metalled road at Taüll; take this road back to Boi (1260m/4134ft).

A shorter alternative to this long last day is to finish the walk in the Refugio d'Estany Llong, (1985m/6512ft) via the Dellui pass. You can then take a taxi to Boi.

Glacial erosion has clearly shaped the national park, as is visible around Estany Negre.

TREK 4: TREKKING AROUND THE VAL D'ARAN

Not far from the town of Baqueira lies the Plan de Beret valley and the source of the Río Garona, the main river that flows through the Val d'Aran and into Bordeaux in France to be expelled on the Atlantic coast. The Val d'Aran is one of the most isolated valleys on the Spanish pensinsula and is surrounded by some of Spain's highest peaks. Due to this isolation the dense forests still harbour a rich variety of wildlife, including the rare Brown bear.

TREK ESSENTIALS

LENGTH: 7 days; 101km (60½ miles).
ACCESS: The easiest and fastest way to get to Vielha and the Val d'Aran is from Zaragoza, via Huesca or Lerida, and then on the N230 through the Túnel de Vielha.
DIFFICULTY: Strenuous.
HIGHEST POINT: Tuc der Ôme 2703m (8868ft).
TREK STYLE: Refuges and bivouacking.
MAPS: Editorial Alpina Val d'Aran.
FURTHER OPTIONS: None.

Our starting point for this trek is the capital town of the Val d'Aran, Vielha (1000m/3281ft). Vielha has grown considerably due to increased tourism within the last few years, it is now possible to purchase all necessary provisions here and accommodation of every conceivable type is available; Vielha is even one of the holiday locations of the King of Spain.

Vielha to Refugio dera Honeria

From this small town, romantically set in attractive mountains, head in a northerly direction, following the left bank of the Río Garona downstream. Leaving the village behind, follow a wide track (the GR211) through woodland until you reach the village of Es Bòrdes (850m/2789ft). This picturesque hamlet has fine examples of traditional vernacular architecture, with all of the houses constructed from hand-crafted local stone.

Continue through the village and out the other side, still following the course of the river. With each twist and turn in the path, new vistas reveal themselves and small clusters of houses and barns cling to the plunging hillsides. After a further hour the path crosses a road bridge and continues along the other side of the river. Eventually you will reach the village of Bahns de Les. About 1½km (1 mile) beyond the village, the river is once again crossed and after a walk along the road there is a junction (600m/1968ft), where you turn right to

Fantastic views of the Val d'Aran and the glacier on distant Pico Aneto can be seen from the village of Baquèira on a clear day.

The Upper Río Garona flows through the Val d'Aran, passing close by the village of Es Bórdes.

valley that lies ahead in an easterly direction for about 7km (4¼ miles) up to Refugio dera Honeria (1015m/3330ft).

If time is limited it's possible to save a day's walking by driving all the way up to Refugio dera Honeria.

Refugio dera Horneria to Casas des Mines de Liat

Directly in front of the refuge the GR211 heads off in a north-easterly direction along the banks of the Gòrges d'Ermer stream. After approximately 30 minutes a small reservoir is passed and after a further 2km (1¼ miles) the route turns towards the south-east and goes steeply up the valley ahead. After an exhausting 1000-m (3280-ft) ascent, the Pasada de Güerri pass is finally reached. (2325m/7628ft). The path now starts to descend gently; down below on the left are the crystal-clear waters of numerous glacial lakes. Ahead are some semi-ruined buildings (2300m/ 7546ft), remnants from the mining era, where a bivouac can be set up for the night. As the evening draws in, there are stunning views over the Rasos de Liat valley, culminating with the sun setting on the Tuc de La Sèrra Nauta and surrounding peaks.

Canejan. Cross the bridge and take the path that leads off the road on the left-hand side, following the GR211 as it zigzags its way up to the village (900m/2953ft). From Canejan, follow the

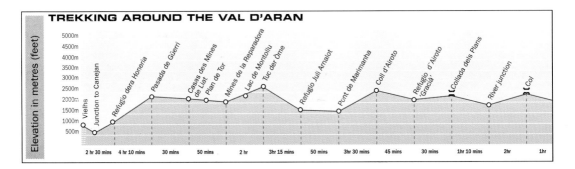

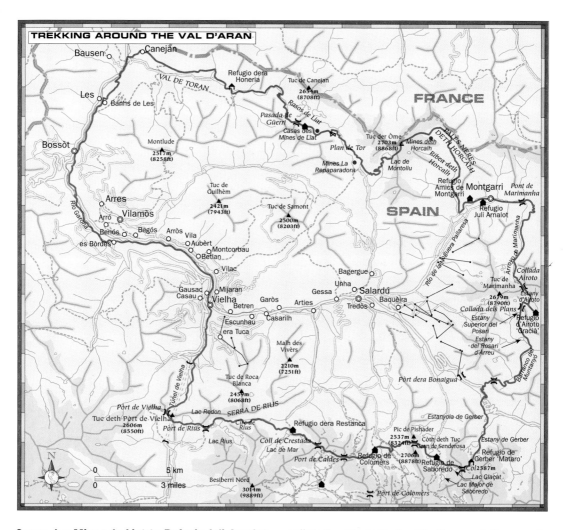

TREKKING AROUND THE VAL D'ARAN

Casas des Mines de Liat to Refugio Juli Arnalot

Weather permitting, today offers some wonderful scenery. After perhaps a chilly night, the first warming rays of sunlight will be more than welcome. However, don't waste too much time as an exhausting day in this exciting part of the Pyrenees lies ahead. Follow the path down the valley in an easterly direction and then walk down to the wide open valley of Plan de Tor (2100m/6890ft).

After crossing the valley above the deserted La Reparadora mines, make the ascent to Lac de Montollu (2350m/7710ft). Walk round the lake in an anti-clockwise direction and on reaching the

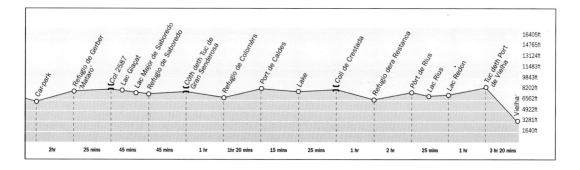

The first autumn snows cap Tuc d'Orla, whose peak rises above the Montgarri valley.

eastern bank head north-east up a short but steep valley to gain the southern slopes of the Tuc der Òme (2703m/8868ft), which is climbed easily to the top. From here there are breathtaking views over the whole Val d'Aran, and large parts of the French Pyrenees can also be seen.

Continue in a north-easterly direction and descend gently until you join the valley of the Ribea deth Horcalh river. Descend the valley on a rocky path, which soon enters alpine pastures and eventually a forest. After about 5 hours of walking a small bridge is encountered along with some deserted houses; just before the bridge turn to join a bigger path and follow the Río de Noguera Pallaresa several hundred metres downstream until you reach the Refugio Amics de Montgarri by an old church. On the other side of the river is the newer Refugio Juli Arnalot (1650m/5413ft).

Refugio Juli Arnalot to Refuge d'Airoto 'Gracià'

Leave the refuge and follow the track along the side of the atmospheric Río de Noguera Pallaresa valley. Dense coniferous forests of pine and spruce alternate with mysterious clearings and innumerable cascading streams. It is still possible to hear the call of the rare black woodpecker and capercaillie during the spring in these extensive woods. After about 3km (2 miles) a little bridge, Pont de Marimanha, is reached (1585m/5200ft) and just beyond in a clearing a little path heads off to the right, up the side of a hill and back into the forest. The path soon joins the course of the Arroyo de Marimanha river.

At a height of about 2000m (6562ft) the woods give way to alpine pasture, which is crossed still following the river. In this area you may well see chamoix, and where they are to be found the golden eagle is usually not too far away. A particularly good time to see the eagles is in the early morning or evenings when they are searching for prey.

Leaving this alpine pasture behind, the route now veers south and enters a valley strewn with fallen trees and giant boulders. After reaching a little lake continue with some difficulty up a scree slope to the Coll d'Airoto pass (2599m/8527ft), where the landscape changes from one of rounded hills to rugged and jaggy peaks. From the pass, head for the small, unmanned Refugio d'Airoto 'Gracià' on the southern edge of the Estany d'Airoto (2197m/7208ft).

Refugio d'Airoto 'Gracià' to Refugio de Saboredo

From the refuge, backtrack along the lake for about 10 minutes and then continue in a north-westerly direction to climb the short ascent to the Collada dels Plans. From here turn towards the south and descend the high-lying valley until you are about 0.5km (⅓ mile) beyond the second lake. The way on heads off to the right and follows the Barranco del Muntanyó up the valley to the south-west. Follow the valley and eventually climb the ridge at its end (2350m/7710ft). From the ridge there are awesome views of Pico Aneto 30km (18 miles) to the west, which is the highest mountain on Spanish territory after Mount Teide in the Canary Islands. Below, the popular Pòrt dera Bonaigua ski resort can be seen.

Descend to the road below and follow it to the car-park and tourist information centre. The path now contours round the side of a hill in a souther-ly direction for about 1km (⅔ mile). A short ascent then leads to a little lake (2071m/6795ft). Follow the path up the valley past the larger Estany de

A rich variety of deciduous and evergreen trees make up the woodland of the Val d'Aran.

THE MINING INDUSTRY

In the last hundred years the Val d'Aran and neighbouring French Vallèe de Lez were known for their mining industry, based mainly on zinc and silver deposits. The mines were located at a height of between 1700m (5570ft) and 2500m (8200ft); this forced the miners to live the majority of the year in the high mountains. To this day the remains of old mining huts are still visible as a testament to the hardy folk who worked in these arduous conditions.

The raw ore was brought down from the mountains by a combination of sledges, hydraulic ramps, mules, railways and even cableways (a lift for buckets) to the crushing plants known as *bocards*. The ore was than processed in villages on both sides of the border.

The pace at which the zinc mines functioned was based on the varying market value over the last century and was strongly affected by both world wars. In the second half of the 20th century several attempts were made to make the failing industry lucrative once again, but the uneconomic method of extraction meant the end for most of these mines. Nowadays, only a few companies are still in operation on the Spanish side of the Pyrenees.

Gerber lake and continue on to the unmanned Refugio de Gerber 'Matoro' (2474m/81117ft). Behind the refuge head south-west and climb a steep scree slope until you arrive at a pass (2587m/8488ft). From here the Refugio de Saboredo can be seen below. Descend the steep slope down past Lac Glaçat (2490m/8169ft) and Lac Major de Saboredo (2339m/7674ft) to reach the manned refuge (2310m/7579ft).

Refugio de Saboredo to Refugio dera Restanca

From the refuge walk towards the north-west and climb to the Tuc Gran de Senderosa col, which lies between Tuc Gran de Senderosa and Pic de Pishader. Down below can be seen the sparkling waters of countless lakes. Descend into the beau-tiful Colomèrs valley and on meeting the GR11 turn right. Continue along the way-marked GR11 past the Refugio de Colomèrs, through the Port de Caldes (2567m/8422ft) and Coll de Crestada (2472m/8110ft) passes, down to the manned Refugio dera Restanca (2010m/6594ft).

A giant pine tree acts as a landmark on the route through the Marimanha valley.

Refugio dera Restanca to Vielha

Today the route continues to follow the GR11. Head up the valley that is dominated by the jagged edged Sierra De Rius. You will eventually reach Lac Rius (2238m/7343ft), which is passed on the northern side.

On reaching the south-western end of the lake, ascend to the Pòrt de Rius pass (2344m/7690ft). From here take the path that rises in a north-westerly direction to a small saddle less than a kilometre away. From the saddle Lac Redon is visible below, with the Tuc deth Pòrt de Vielha (2606m/8550ft) peak mirrored in its waters. Descend to the lake and then ascend the Tuc Deth Pòrt de Vielha via its eastern slopes on a slightly vague track. From the summit turn right onto a better path that heads north-west and quickly joins the GR211. Easily descend through a valley, passing a little chapel before crossing a stream. Continue along a forested path and after nearly 2km (1⅓ miles) you will join a farm track. Follow the farm track for 3km (1¾ miles) back to Vielha.

In alpine meadows such as this in the Upper Marimanha valley chamoix can often be spotted.

TREK 5: VALLE DE GISTAIN

Over five days this classic tour circumnavigates Pico Posets (3375m/11073ft) in the second highest massif of the Pyrenees. The trek follows the picturesque valley of the Río Zinqueta up to its source and then, after crossing the Peurto de Gistain with its marvellous views of the surrounding three-thousanders, descends into the Estós Valley (Vall d'Estós) and up the Arroyo de Batisielles. The trek also offers the possibility to climb Pico Posets before returning back into the Valle de Gistain and San Juan de Plan.

The Río Zinqueta flows through the fertile Valle de Gistain.

TREK ESSENTIALS

LENGTH: 5 days; 54km (32 miles).
ACCESS: San Juan de Plan is best accessed from Lleida or Huesca on the N240 via Barbastro. From Barbastro, take the N123, then the N138 to Salinas de Sin and the A2609 to San Juan de Plan.
DIFFICULTY: Moderate to strenuous.
HIGHEST POINT: Collado de Eriste (2860m/9383ft).
TREK STYLE: Refuges and/or camping.
MAPS: Editorial Alpina 1: 25 000 Posets; Editorial Alpina 1: 25 000 Bachimala.
FURTHER OPTIONS: Climb Pico Posets (3375m/11073ft) – crampons and ice-axe required.

This trek should only be done by experienced hill walkers as there are considerable height gains to overcome and route finding can be problematic.

San Juan de Plan to Refugio de Vaidós

In the small medieval mountain village of San Juan de Plan (1120m/3675ft), where it is possible to purchase provisions, try to make time to visit the local ethnological museum. The museum is located in a former abbey and has fine examples of the tools, clothing, musical instruments, toys and cooking implements used by past inhabitants of the Valle de Gistain

From the village, follow the road towards Gistain for about 1km (⅔ mile) before taking a track that

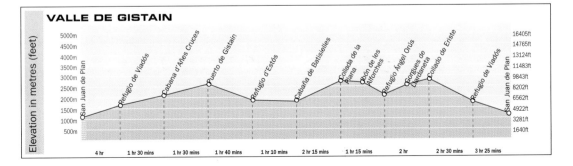

VALLE DE GISTAIN

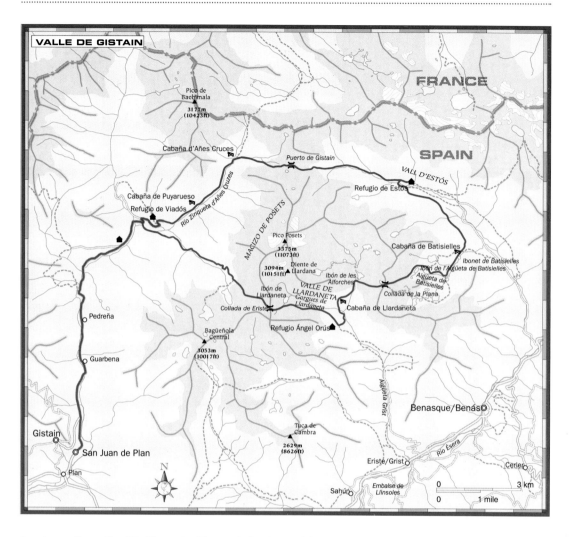

heads north up the Río Zinqueta. The path leads through a fertile valley surrounded by pastures, where the hedgerows of sloe bushes are frequent-ed by stonechats and red-backed shrikes. In the dense vegetation along the sides of the Valle de Gistain live hawks, sparrow-hawks and booted eagles. The crystal-clear waters of the Río Zinqueta are the hunting ground of otters, dippers and the rare Pyrenean desman.

As the valley gains height the scenery changes to pine forest, which offers welcome shade on a hot summer's day. After 12km (7¼ miles) the Refugio de Vaidós (1745m/5725ft) is found in a small clearing; if the refuge is full, or if you prefer to camp, tents can be pitched next to the refuge, but always ask the warden first. Pico Posets and the adjacent glacier shimmer in the evening light.

Shrikes (*Larius collurio*) inhabit the indigenous sloe bushes of the Valle de Gistain.

Then, as stillness sweeps into the valley, only the call of an occasional owl breaks the silence.

Refugio de Vaidós to Refugio de Estós

Leave the hut following the GR11-marked path in a north-westerly direction. The river, which will be on your right-hand side, soon leads to the Cabaña de Puyarueso on the other side of the valley on the tree-line. After about 1½ hours of walking another hut, Cabaña d'Añes Cruces (2050m/6726ft), is reached. From here, cross the brook and head west up the valley. Looking back, you will see the impressive massif of Pico de Bachimala, also known as Pic Schrader (3177m/10423ft).

Carry on up the valley to Puerto de Gistain (2595m/ 8514ft). From here the panorama opens out in a westerly direction and, in good weather, there are some fine views of Pico de Aneto (3404m/ 11168ft), the highest peak in the Pyrenees. Also remarkable here are the 'simas', deep shafts formed in the limestone by glacial melt-water, some of which reach depths of over 500m (1640ft) and are a potholer's paradise.

Beyond the pass the route descends across scree to enter the Vall d'Estós, where the Refugio de Estós (1895m/6217ft) is located.

Refugio de Estós to Refugio Ángel Orús

From the refuge the route crosses to the other side of the valley, where a way-marked path contours west across the hillside. At 1900m (6234ft), and after just over an hour's walk, a small barn, Cabaña de Batisielles, is passed. Turning to the south-west, the trek now follows a small splashing brook up the valley ahead. After approximately another hour, you will reach a group of small tarns, which are supplied by the waters of the Aigüeta de Batisielles. This is only the

Pine trees edge a glacial lake in the Posets Massif.

beginning of a whole series of small, natural lakes to be found on the eastern slopes of the Pico Posets.

At this first group of lakes turn eastwards and follow the brook further up. On reaching the Ibon de l'Aigüeta de Batisielles, go round the right-hand side of the lake and climb the rocky path that heads west to the Collada de la Plana (2702m/ 8865ft). From the pass you will be able to see Refugio Ángel Orús ahead – it sits below one of the spurs of the Posets massif and is dominated by the colossal and seemingly unconquerable Pico Posets (3375m/11073ft).

Continue downwards across steep terrain to the Ibón de Grist, also known as Ibón de les Alforches (2411m/7910ft). Cross the stream and descend a path to the left, then head diagonally to the right of the valley. On reaching a small hut (Cabaña de Llardaneta) the path goes straight down to the valley bottom, and after crossing another small stream some marvellous waterfalls appear on the left. It is only a few steps up to the manned Refugio Ángel Orús (2100m/6890ft).

Refugio Ángel Orús to San Juan de Plan
Leave the refuge, following the same route as if

you were heading for Pico Posets (see Peak box below), up to the Gorgues de Llardaneta (2585m/8481ft). However, instead of crossing the river, turn west towards the Ibón de Llardaneta, which you pass on its left-hand side, before climbing to Collado de Eriste (2860m/9383ft). The pass, which is reached after some 2 hours of walking, opens out onto lovely views along the Valle de Gistain. The path now descends over rocky terrain, followed by alpine pastures and, eventually, sparse pine woods, until reaching Refugio de Viadós.

From the refuge retrace your steps from the first day of the trek back to San Juan de Plan.

PEAK: PICO POSETS

The easiest way of ascending Pico Posets is from the Refugio Ángel Orús. Please note that, although only graded as a scramble, crampons and ice-axe are essential tools for conquering this peak.

Leave the refuge and take the well-marked path, parallel to some old water channels, up the slope. The route crosses alpine pastures strewn with rock cuboids to reach the Gorgues de Llardaneta after 1¼ hours.

Ford the river in a north-north-westerly direction, and continue up the slope for about 10 minutes. The trail turns right into the Canal Fonda gully (2630m/8629ft). Throughout most of the year snow and ice is present here, hence the need for crampons and ice-axe. The gully

At 3375m (11073ft), Pico Posets is the second highest peak in the Pyrenees, after Pico de Aneto (3404m/11168ft).

quickly gains height and ends at a col where, on the left, is the peculiar rock formation of Diente de Llardaneta, which at 3085m (10121ft) is a three-thousander that can be bagged from the col in only a few minutes.

The way on, however, heads up the steep and somewhat loose ridge all the way to the summit. It might be worth using a rope on this section to safeguard against a fall. A spectacular panorama awaits from the summit. Descend via the same route.

CLIMB ESSENTIALS

SUMMIT Pico Posets 3375m (11073ft).
CAMP Refugio Ángel Orús.
GRADE Scramble Grade 1 (ice-axe and crampons necessary).

EASTERN (CATALUNIAN) PYRENEES DIRECTORY

GETTING THERE

By air: Barcelona and Toulouse (France) are the most convenient airports for the Catalunian Pyrenees. These airports are served by many different airlines including British Airways, BMI British Midland and Iberia. The high season for tickets is July and August, Easter and Christmas. If you're booking quite far in advance, look out for cheap deals on Easy Jet, Go and Ryanair.
BMI (British Midland): www.britishmidlands.com
British Airways: www.britishairways.com
Easy Jet: www.easyjet.com
Go Airlines: www.go-fly.com
Iberia Airlines: www.iberia.com
Ryanair: www.ryanair.com

By train: A train service runs from Lleida to Pobla de Segur, the main access point for the Catalunian Pyrenees, on specific dates from February to October. The train is also available for charter throughout the year. To confirm train times, contact:
ARMF, Apartado de Correos 62, tel: 973 290795, fax: 973 290 916.
Girona Train Station: Plaza de España; tel. 972 207093
RENFE, Barcelona: tel. 93 4900202

By bus: There is a regular service operated by Alsina Graells from Barcelona and Lleida, stopping at Pobla de Segur and Llavorsí. To confirm bus times, contact:
Alsina Graells: Pobla de Segur; tel: 973 680336
Alsina Graells: Lleida; tel: 973 271470
Alsina Graells: Barcelona; tel: 93 2656866.
Girona Bus Station: Plaza de España; tel. 972 212319

ACCOMMODATION

Refuge Information: www.refugiosyalbergues.com

Manned Refuges

Albergue El Molino (San Juan de Plan): tel. 974 506212
Albergue La Fraga (Queralbs): tel. 972 727388
Albergue Pic de l'Àliga (Núria) (2122m/6962ft): 138 places; tel. 972 730048
Refugio Ángel Orús (2100m/6890ft): 50 places; tel. 974 344044
Refugio Amics de Montgarri (1657m/5436ft): 50 places; open 1 December to 30 April and 25 May to 20 October; tel. 973 645064 or 973 640780; email kimcalbeto@hotmail.com
Refugio Coma de Vaca (2000m/6562ft): 42 places; open during Easter and from 15 June to 15 September (also open in winter if they receive enough bookings); tel. 972 198082/936 824237
Refugio de Colomèrs (2130m/6988ft): 40 places; open mid-June to October; tel. 973 253008

Refugio de Estós (1890m/6201ft): 185 places; open all year round; tel. 974 551483
Refugio Juli Arnalot (1650m/5413ft): 14 places; open all year; tel. 608 998436
Refugio Lluis Estasen (1640m/5381ft): 90 places; open in summer; tel. 938 220079/908 315312
Refugio CEC La Molina: tel.972 892005/699 927937
Refugio Prat d'Aguiló (2037m/6683ft): 35 places; open over Easter and from 1 June to 30 October; tel. 973 250135
Refugio de La Restanca (2010m/6594ft): 80 places; open June to end September and weekends; tel. 908 036559/ 973 680702
Refugio de Saboredo (2310m/7579ft): 18 places; open in summer; tel. 973 253015/93 3299736
Refugio Ventosa i Galvell (2222m/7290ft): 80 places; tel. 973 297090
Refugio de Viadós (1700m/5578ft): 65 places; open weekends in spring and from 20 June to 30 September; tel. 974 506163

Unmanned Refuges

Refugio dera Honeira (1015m/3330ft)
Refugio d'Arioto 'Gracià' (2203m/7223ft); 10 places; open all year

TOURIST INFORMATION

Catalunia Tourist Office: Rambla de la Llibertat, 1, Girona; tel. 972 226575
National Park Administration: tel. 938 244151

Benasque: tel. 974 551289
Bielsa: tel. 974 308350
Gòsol: tel. 973 370055
Josa de Cadí and Tiuxèn: tel. 973 370030
Lleida: Avda Madrid 36; tel. 973 270997
Pedraforca Information Centre: tel. 938 258005
Ribes de Freser: tel. 972 727728
Saldes: tel. 938 258005
Valle de Núria: tel. 972 732020
Vielha: C/Sarriulera 10; tel. 973 640110

EMERGENCY SERVICES:

Emergency Service/Mountain Rescue: tel. 112
Catalunia Weather Information: tel. 906 365906/906 330033/93 2125766; www.gencat.es/servmet/pirineu/index.htm
Avalanche Warning Service: tel. 934 232572/934 232967

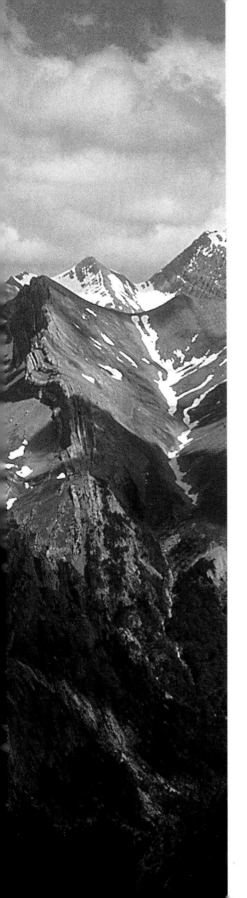

5

WESTERN (ARAGONES -NAVARRO) PYRENEES

The Western (Aragones– Navarro) Pyrenees are wild and abrupt in contrast to the more gentle and ordered eastern part of the mountain range. Aragón is sometimes called the land of giants – 10 of the 12 tallest peaks in peninsular Spain can be found here. Despite such unforgiving terrain, the region is home to the magnificent Ordesa and Monte Perdido National Park and hundreds of fascinating towns and villages, rich in both tradition and history.

Looking east from the Estribiella col, the mighty peak of Bisaurin rises above the forested Selva de Oza (trek 8).

This remote area situated between the provinces of Aragón and Navarra is the true start of the alpine Pyrenees. From the plain of the Río Aragón, the mountains rise gently until they reach an elevation of 2662m (8734ft). Due to this natural rock barrier, the valleys situated on the southern side are protected against bad weather prevailing from the north-west and have a fundamentally drier climate than the areas further to the west.

Today, these remote valleys are among the least populated in Spain and one of the most delightful seasons for a visit to this area is during the autumn months, when the beech forests transform themselves into a myriad of hues. Bright yellows through to deep reds form the carpet of freshly fallen leaves on the forest floor and walking through these vibrant woods, backlit by the autumn sun, leaves a lasting memory.

Local Flora

As the forests give way to alpine pastures, the countryside, transformed into a scene of lush green fields separated by small rocky protrusions jutting skywards, provides the habitat for a wide variety of flowers, and for every colour there is a butterfly to match. Further west in Navarra the area is typified by sleepy mountain villages surrounded by immense woodlands, part natural, partly cultivated. The foothills of this, the western extremity of the Pyrenees, rise gently to over 1500m (4920ft) in height and because of the humid climate, consist of extensive dense forests through which run clear rivers and streams and throughout the whole year provide vital feeders for the Río Ebro further south.

The alpine meadows are good places for spotting rare butterflies, such as this Silver-washed fritillary.

Bielsa

One of the area's most attractive towns is Bielsa. Although it may feel like a medieval mountain town, with its quaint arcaded plazas, in actual fact only Bielsa's church, bridge and town hall precede the Spanish Civil War of 1936–39. After the Republican army had retreated from the plains in the spring of 1938, it took up positions in Pyrenean towns such as Barbastra, Benasque and Bielsa. The Nationalist forces, however, pursued the army into the mountains and seized the surrounding towns and villages one by one. By June the Republicans were isolated in Bielsa, with the Puerto Biello into France their only escape route. The Republicans managed to hold their ground until 16 June, when the Nationalists subjected the town to an especially fierce bombardment. With the town engulfed in flames, the Republican army had no choice but to retreat still further.

Ordesa and Monte Perdido National Park

Bielsa, along with Ainsa to the south (which possesses more authentic medieval architecture), is an excellent base for exploring the Ordesa and Monte Perdido National Park. Established in the Valle de Ordesa by royal decree in 1918, the park has expanded tenfold over the years to 156 square kilometres (60 square miles) and now encompasses Monte Perdido and large portions of the Pineta, Escuain and Añisclo valleys. The park is well known for its forests of firs and beeches and its abundant protected wildlife. Golden eagles, griffon vultures, capercaillies, wild boar, otters and a healthy number of chamoix can all be spotted here. Unfortunately, the Spanish ibex (*el bucardo*) which once thrived throughout the Pyrenees and Cordillera Cantábrica and then for many years could only be found in the Valle de Ordesa, is now on the brink of extinction.

Jaca

Just west of the Parque Nacional de Ordesa y Monte Perdido is the busy town of Jaca. Dating back to the 2nd century, Jaca was an important stop on the pilgrims' route to Santiago de Compostela and, in 1035, also became the first capital of the kingdom of Aragón. Many of Aragón's early kings are buried nearby at the Monasterio de San Juan de la Peña, tucked under the brow of a cliff on the Pano Mountain. This small tract of land has been the site of a monastery for nearly a thousand years. The first monastery, constructed in about 920, was responsible for introducing the Latin mass to Spain. In 1071 it was replaced by a

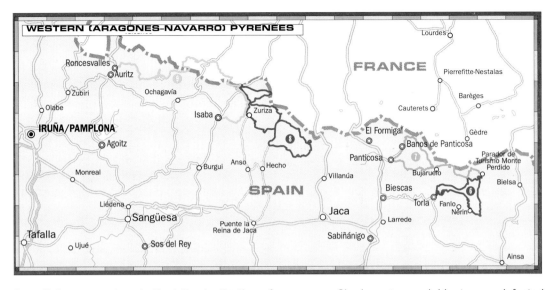

Benedictine monastery, built at the instigation of Sancho Ramírez, son of King Ramiro I. Both Sancho Ramírez and his father are buried at the monastery and are honoured in the pantheon adjoining the monastery's church.

The Spirit of Navarra

Aragón's western neighbour, Navarra, may lack the former's spectacular peaks, but it, too, could be called a land of giants. Navarra is home to one of the most fiercely independent societies in Spain and can also lay claim to some of the most enduring dramas in Western mythology. The death of Roland at the historic pass of Roncesvalles was played out here in the 8th century, and every year the city of Pamplona, which lies on the southern fringe of the mountain range, hosts the famous running with the bulls of the San Fermín fiesta.

Though Navarra has at various times in the past fallen to the French, Aragonese and Castilians, foreign domination of the region has never lasted for long. Indeed until the mid-19th century, Navarra was a separate kingdom with special rights, or *fueros*, including its own parliament, currency and system of taxes. Even during the Franco regime, when expressions of local identity were suppressed throughout the rest of Spain, Navarra retained a degree of autonomy. Navarra is today officially a province of Spain – but in the country's modern, decentralized state, the ancient kingdom is still very much a region apart.

Navarra's spirited self-sufficiency has of course led to ferocious battles throughout the centuries. Perhaps the most famous of these took place at Roncesvalles in the 8th century. After the Frankish emperor Charlemagne and his troops defeated Pamplona and demolished the city's walls, they retreated north through the Ibañeta Pass. Much of Charlemagne's army had a safe journey, but the rearguard – including the Frankish hero Roland – was ambushed and slaughtered by Basques as it marched through the pass (see page 78).

Roland's legendary last stand took place just outside the Valle de Aézkoa, one of nine picturesque valleys — each dotted with towns and villages – in the Navarran Pyrenees. The communities in the Valle de Roncal, the Navarro Pyrenees' easternmost valley, are famous both for their ewe's cheese and their rafters, or *almadieros*, who skilfully transport tree trunks to sawmills on the valley's swiftly flowing rivers.

The Selva de Irati in the Western Pyrenees is full of numerous small streams and waterfalls.

TREK 6: THE ORDESA AND MONTE PERDIDO NATIONAL PARK

Without doubt, one of the best-known areas of the Spanish Pyrenees is the Ordesa and Monte Perdido National Park, which offers some of the most impressive landscapes in this beautiful mountain range. Both the Ordesa and Monte Perdido National Park and the Covadonga National Park in Asturias were founded in 1918, the first national parks to be created in Spain. At the beginning of the last century the Ordesa Valley (Valle de Ordesa) was as yet undiscovered by Spanish and foreign travellers alike, but within a few decades had become well known throughout Spain. The Ordesa and Monte Perdido National Park is currently the most frequented park in Spain. Covering an area of about 156 square kilometres, the Ordesa Valley, along with the Añisclo Valley (Valle de Añisclo) to the south and the Pineta Valley (Valle de Pineta) to the east, is characterized by deep ravines cut into the Perdido massif. This rugged beauty makes the Central Pyrenees and, especially, this distinctive national park unique experiences.

TREK ESSENTIALS

LENGTH: 3 days; 58km (36¼ miles).
ACCESS: To get to Torla, take the road from Huesca on the N330 to Sabiñánigo and Biescas and then the N260 to Torla.
DIFFICULTY: Moderate to strenuous.
HIGHEST POINT: 2700m (8859ft).
TREK STYLE: Refuges and a bunkhouse.
MAPS: Editorial Alpina 1:25 000 Ordesa y Monte Perdido.
FURTHER OPTIONS: A shortcut can be taken from the Collado Superior de Arrablo down Fuen Blanca to shorten the second day of the trek by 2 hours.

Torla to Refugio de Gòriz

The starting point for this trek is 7km (4¼ miles) beyond the village of Torla at the car-park at La Pradera de Ordesa. (1320m/4331ft). In the summer months, all vehicles except taxis and buses are prohibited from driving along this last section of road. The trek can be started in Torla itself, or a taxi or bus can be taken to the end of the road.

From La Pradera de Ordesa a well-marked path heads off up the deep, wide and once-glaciated valley, following the course of the Río Arazas. Along the wooded path are breathtaking views of the surrounding mountain scenery and, with a little luck, red crossbills might also be seen. After about an hour, the first of numerous waterfalls comes into view – all of the falls make excellent photo opportunities. On passing the Gradas de Soaso waterfall (1700m/5577ft) the valley gradually narrows until it abruptly ends at the Circo de Soaso. The route now crosses the river on a small wooden bridge and then climbs out of the valley on a zigzagging path. Looking to the opposite side of the valley you will see the Cola de Caballo waterfall which, as its name suggests, resembles a horse's tail.

After approximately an hour's climb the top edge of the valley is reached at 2000m (6562ft). The path now continues to gain a further 200m (650ft) of height until it reaches Refugio de Gòriz (also known as Refugio Delgado Úbeda) (2195m/7201ft). The refuge is situated at the foot of Monte Perdido and offers a stunning, high

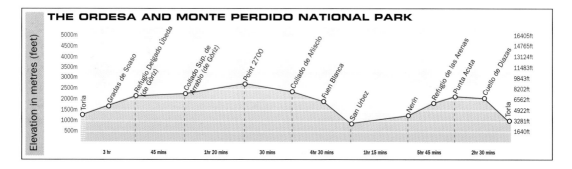

mountain panorama. Reaching a height of 3355m (11008ft), Monte Perdido (Lost Mountain) is not only the highest limestone elevation in Europe, but is also recognized by many as one of the most beautiful peaks in the Pyrenees. An interesting feature of the area is the remains of the Monte Perdido Glacier. Situated on the north-eastern side of the Perdido massif, this glacier once filled the whole of the Valle de Pineta. Unfortunately, over the last 10 years, along with other glaciers in the Pyrenees, it has shrunk to about half of its size.

As dusk approaches, chamoix or even the rare Iberian ibex may be spotted grazing on the alpine pastures. These are the few remaining examples of the extremely rare Iberian ibex. Unlike the ill-fated Pyrenean ibex, whose last female was found dead in January 2000, this shy little creature still has a chance of survival.

The impressive Añisclo gorge has cut a path more than a thousand metres deep into the limestone landscape.

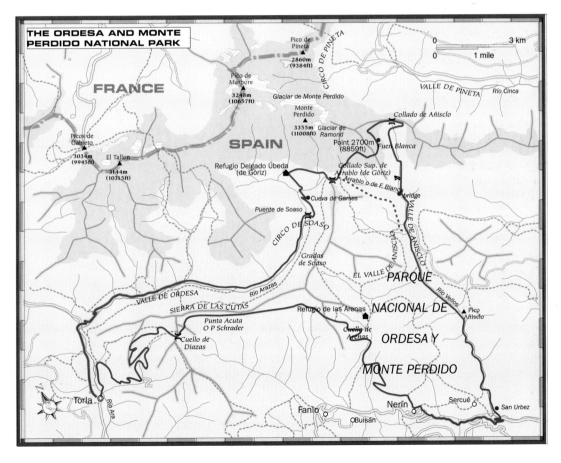

THE ORDESA AND MONTE PERDIDO NATIONAL PARK

Refugio de Gòriz to Nerín

Set off from the Refugio de Gòriz following the GR11 eastwards to the Collado Superior de Arrablo (2343m/7687ft), which is reached after approximately 45 minutes. The less experienced walker could now continue straight down the Fuen Blanca Valley to rejoin the main route in the Río Vellos (Añisclo) valley. However, the trek continues to follow the GR11 further round the Monte Perdido massif on a slightly exposed rocky path. On reaching the Collado de Añisclo (2456m/8058ft) there are overwhelming views of the Valle de Pineta to the north and the Valle de Añisclo to the south.

The charcteristic rock forms of the Valle de Ordesa glow in the evening light.

Turn right at the col and enter the Valle de Añisclo, and then follow the river downstream. After passing the Fuen Blanca spring (1900m/ 6234ft) the route enters the long and deep Añisclo gorge. Follow the gorge for 10km (6 miles) until you reach the small chapel of San Urbez (900m/ 2953ft) embedded in a rock face. At the chapel you must cross the Río Vellos one last time on a lofty stone bridge. The path now leads directly to the Fanlo–Escalonia road. At the road turn right in the direction of Fanlo. Follow the road for 3.5km (2¼ miles) until you reach a junction – turn right and you will soon arrive at the small, picturesque, mountain village of Nerín (1280m/4199ft). The only accommodation here is in the *albergue* (bunkhouse).

FLORA OF THE VALLE DE ORDESA

The Valle de Ordesa is covered with spruce and pine (*Pinaceae*), beech (*Fagaceae*) and some isolated oaks (*Quercus*). It is typical of these woods that the spruce predominates on the shady northern side, while on the sunny southern slopes grow beech and even mountain pine (*Pinus mugo*). The sub-growth is mainly made up of rhododendron (*Rhododendron ferrugineum*), blueberries (*Vaccinium*), raspberries (*Rubus idaeus*) and wild strawberries (*Fragaria vesca*). Also to be found is the limestone-adoring small yellow foxglove (*Digitalis lutea*) and different kinds of orchid (*Dactylorhiza*) (see picture).

Protected from the elements, the deep gorges on the southern side are subject to a fundamentally damp, warmer climate and a vast wealth of plants flourishes. Up to an altitude of approximately 1500m (4920ft) grow large-leaved limes (*Tilia platyphyllos*), ash (*Fraxinus*

excelsior) and the wych elm (*Ulmus glabra*).

In the higher parts of the valleys are meadows, which are used as alpine pastures for cattle and sheep during the summer months. In the spring, after the thaw, the rare common pasque flower (*Pulsatilla vulgaris*), crocus (*Crocus vernus*) and Pyrenean buttercup (*Ranunculus pyrenaeus*) all grow in these meadows. Later, in the summer, yellow and alpine gentians (*Gentiana nivalis*), narcissi (*Narcissus*) and the endemic, splendidly violet-coloured Pyrenean lily (*Lilium pyrenaicum*) bloom. On the steep rock faces, whether in the shady damp gorges or in the glistening sun, interesting plants thrive everywhere.

In addition to this profusion of plant life, the Valle de Ordesa's remote and inaccessible situation has enabled many species of animal to survive, such as the Pyrenean desman (*Galemys pyrenaicus*), otters (*Lutra lutra*) and various species of birds, from wallcreepers (*Tichodromadidae*) to Bearded vultures, otherwise known as lammergeiers (*Gypaëtus barbatus*), and Eagle owls (*Bubo bubo*), which in other areas had already become rare or even extinct by the beginning of the last century.

PEAK: MONTE PERDIDO

CLIMB ESSENTIALS

SUMMIT: Monte Perdido 3355m (11007ft).
CAMP: Refugio de Gòriz.
GRADE: Scramble Grade 1.

Monte Perdido is a fairly straightforward peak, although an ice axe could prove useful if you embark on it before the end of August.

Take the vague path from behind Refugio de Gòriz; this quickly improves and is marked with cairns throughout most of its length. The route scrambles up through moraine deposits until it reachs the small tarn of Lago Helado (Frozen Lake). This tarn is one of several in the Monte Perdido massif, and it lies exactly between the Perdido and Cilindro peaks. Turn right at the

tarn, and take the ridge to the right of the snow- and ice-filled gully. Higher up, the route moves left into the gully.

Throughout most of the year this area, known as Escupidera (Spittle), is covered with snow or ice, and care must be exercised when crossing this section. On the left is the El Dedo de Perdido pinnacle (3188m/10459ft), shortly after which the route breaks out onto the shoulder just below the summit. The last few metres up to the summit involve climbing loose scree. The marvellous Pyrenean panorama more than compensates for the effort involved in reaching the top.

The way down is by reversing the ascent route.

The mighty Monte Perdido dominates the Valle de Ordesa.

Nerín to Torla

It's wise to leave Nerín fairly early because, although not technically difficult, the last day of the trek is approximately 25km (15 miles) long with a height gain and loss of about 1000m (3280ft).

Leave the village on a forestry track heading north and slowly gaining height through a series of switchbacks. After 3½ hours you will reach the junction up to Refugio de las Arenas (1890m/ 6201ft), where you must turn to the west and start to climb the side of the Sierra de las Cutas. You

will reach the highest point of the sierra, Punta Acuta (2200m/7218ft), after walking for 6 hours. Here, high above the Valle de Ordesa, there are lovely views over the whole region: the complete massif of the Monte Perdido and a large part of the Ordesa and Monte Perdido National Park. From Punta Acuta the route heads down to Cuello de Diazas (2140m/7021ft) and from there down to Torla, deep below in the valley of the Río Ara (1030m/3379ft). The final section of the descent can be shortened by taking the path that cuts through the zigzagging track.

TREK 7: IN THE HEART OF THE PYRENEES

This eight-day tour passes through one of the highest and most demanding parts of the Pyrenees. Not only are the views breathtaking but also the ascents, so it's only recommended for experienced hikers with staying power. The route crosses the Monte Perdido massif into France and passes close by Pic Vignemal on the border. It travels through the impressive glacial valleys of Pineta, Ordesa and Ara and is located in one of the most exciting parts of the Pyrenees. On some days, because of the long distances and lack of refuges, it is necessary to bivouac, so a little planning is required and sufficient provisions must be carried. One night is spent on the French side of the Pyrenees in the Refuge des Sarradets.

TREK ESSENTIALS

LENGTH: 8 days; 100km (60 miles).
ACCESS: Take the N330 from Huesca Barbastro, then the A138 to Ainsa and then on the HU-V-6402 to Bielsa. Turn left in Bielsa to the signposted Parador Turismo de Monte Perido.
DIFFICULTY: Strenuous.
HIGHEST POINT: Cuello de Cilindro 3100m (10171ft).
TREK STYLE: Refuges, camping, bunkhouse and hotel.
MAPS: Editorial Alpina 1:25 000 Ordesa y Monte Perdido, Vignemale Bujaruelo, Panticosa Formigal and Valle de Tena Tendeñera.
FURTHER OPTIONS: The trip can be shortened by finishing at Bujaruelo.

Parador Turismo de 'Monte Perdido' to Lago Helado de Marmoré

The trek begins by the chapel of the Virgin of Pineta, beside the Parador Turismo de 'Monte Perdido' (1290m/4232ft) in the Valle de Pineta. Follow the track, signposted 'Refugio Larri', that heads off in a north-westerly direction from the car-park. After about 3.5km (2¼ miles) a spring with lovely fresh water is found just before a bridge (approximately 1400m/4590ft) over the thundering Río Cinca. A few metres beyond the bridge take the small, but well-marked path that heads north-west and which soon climbs innumerable zigzags to sharply ascend through the Circo de Pineta. With the tree-line now far below, there are open views of the powerful waterfalls of the Río Cinca crashing down.

With the steepest section, El Embudo, now surpassed, you will reach a metal cross on the edge of Balcón de Pineta. Looking back there is a breathtaking panorama of the once-glaciated Valle de Pineta 1300m (4625ft) below. From the *balcón*, the route rises more gently over pastures, where numerous gigantic 'eccentrics' can be seen. These large boulders, sometimes the size of a small building, were deposited during the last ice age. After walking for over 3½ hours you will reach Lago Helado de Marmoré (2595m/8514ft), perched in its surrounding rocky landscape. The Refuge de Tucarroya that sits beside the lake is in a rather regrettable state so it's better to bivouac for the night.

Lago Helado de Marmoré to Refugio Delgado Úbeda (de Gòriz)

Leave the lake and head south up to the base of the Monte Perdido glacier. Three obvious gullys lie in front of you and, depending on the amount of snow, it's best to take either the central or the right-hand one. From the top of the gullies ascend west over the glacier (crampons and ice axe essential) to reach the Cuello del Cilindro pass at 3100m (10171ft). Take the steep rocky track down from the pass to Lago Helado, from where an ascent can be made of Monte Perdido (see

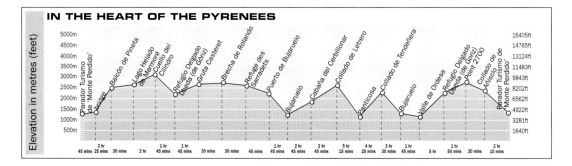

IN THE HEART OF THE PYRENEES

page 67). Descend the zigzagging path down to Refugio Delgado Úbeda (de Gòriz).

Refugio Delgado Úbeda (de Gòriz) to Refuge des Sarradets

From the refuge, take the obvious path north-west. You will follow a gentle valley overlooked by the dominant Perdido massif. After some 45 minutes, on reaching the valley's end, a flat area known as Llano y Cuello de Millaris is entered. It isn't unusual to see vultures and eagles looking for carrion and other prey to plunder in the pastures and rocky crags that shape the landscape. From this somewhat over-grown basin the route gently ascends across scree, past the Collado del Descargador (2457m/ 8061ft), and then up to Gruta Casteret. Gruta Casteret (2773m/9098ft) is an extraordinary ice cave – the highest of its kind to be found anywhere in Europe – and is full of ice formations.

From the ice cave it is a short distance across a small boulder field to the Brecha de Rolando col. This natural rock breach offers an ideal gateway into the nearby Cirque de Garvanie on the French side of the

The wide and wild Río Ara is crossed on the fourth day of this trek.

Pyrenees and has lovely views into both France and Spain. If it's not too busy, chamoix, or even one of the rare ibex, can be spotted here. From the col, it's only a few hundred metres on the well-trodden path across the Brecha glacier down to the manned Refuge des Sarradets (2589m/8495ft).

Refuge des Sarradets to Cabaña del Cerbillonar

As dawn breaks a marvellous light illuminates the nearby Cirque de Gavarnie, which is probably one of the most popular areas in the French Pyrenees due to the numerous waterfalls that plunge, in several stages, into the 2000-m (6560-ft) deep valley; the last stage has an impressive drop of over 300m (980ft). From the hut, take the obvious path through the Col des Sarradets, between the peak of the same name and the Taillon glacier. Follow the path to the Puerto de Bujaruelo (2270m/7448ft), from here you will pass back into Spain on a forestry track that can be followed all

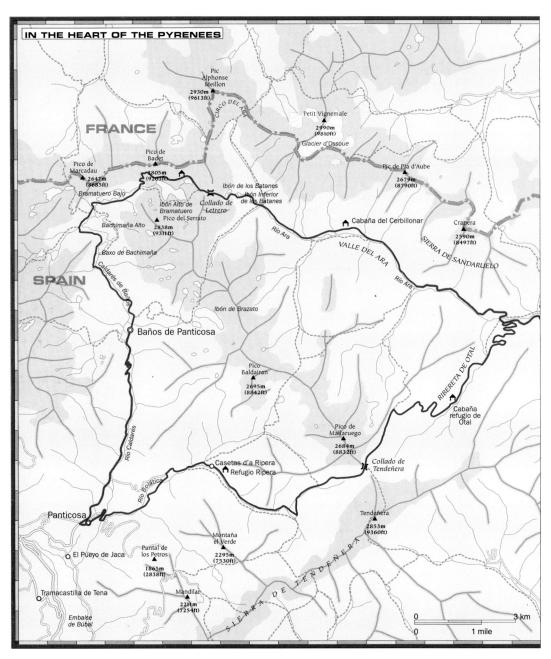

IN THE HEART OF THE PYRENEES

the way down to Bujaruelo. A nicer way of reaching Bujaruelo, however, is on the old path that heads west down the valley of the Barranco Lapazosa, which in the early summer months is a sea of colour due to the thousands of orchids that blossom.

Towards the end of the day you will enter an eerie forest. After crossing the Río Ara on an old roman bridge you will arrive at Bujaruelo. From the Chapel of San Nicolás head along the GR11 on a

jeep track to soon cross the river once again. Continue on to the unmanned Cabaña del Cerbillonar (1800m/5906ft).

Cabaña del Cerbillonar to Panticosa

Try to leave the hut as early as possible as today's final destination, Panticosa, is a considerable distance away with some notable height gains. Follow the Valle del Ara upstream for some 4km (2⅓ miles) until you reach a small shepherd's hut

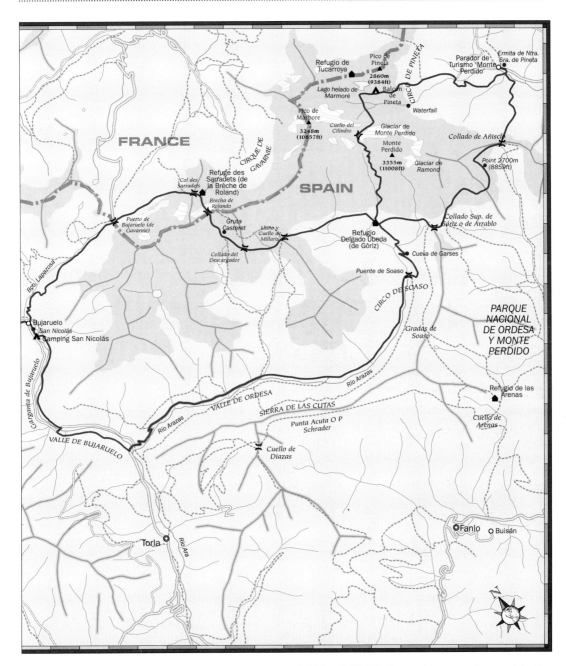

where the GR11 divides. To the east can be seen the towering Pic Vignemale, which had the distinction of being climbed by Lady Lister of Halifax in 1838; to the north lies the Circo del Ara; but the main route of the GR11 goes up a steep slope to the north-west.

Shortly, the first of two small glacial lakes is reached (2270m/7448ft); their icy-cold waters make for a refreshing dip on a hot summer's day. Beyond the lakes lies the Collado de Letrero (2680m/8793ft), from where you descend to the Ibón Alto de Bramatuero reservoir. You can sometimes spot the endemic Pyrenean salamander hiding under small rocks. Reflected in the clear blue waters of the reservoir are the distant peaks of the Infierno range. The route skirts round the right-hand side of the reservoir, and just beyond the dam is a small unmanned refuge. The path continues to descend, now steeply, to the Bramatuero Bajo reservoir and on to the

The peak of El Espolón del Gallinero stands high above the stunning Valle de Ordesa.

Bachimaña Alto reservoir. Descend the Caldarés de Baños valley, past some spectacular waterfalls on the left, and into Baños de Panticosa. Follow the road, or the path above the road, down to the village of Panticosa, where there will be plenty of accommodation, hot water and cold beer awaiting.

Panticosa to Bujaruelo

From the tele-ski lift on the south side of the village a jeep track crosses the Río Caldarés. Just beyond, take the path that turns off to the left and follow the valley of the Río Bolática until you break out onto a jeep track; follow this track all the way to the unmanned Refugio Ripera. From the refuge the route continues along the course of the Río Ripera for a further 3km (1¾ miles) until, at an altitude of 1700m (5577ft) and just before entering the Circo de Ripera, a path turns off to the north-east and climbs up the Barranco del Puerto. This path leads eventually to the Collado de Tendeñera at 2327m (7635ft) – a marvellous panorama awaits, with the Sierra de Tendeñera to

the south and the Monte Perdido massif in the east. Descend into a valley and join a jeep track at the Cabaña refugio de Otal that goes all the way down to Bujaruelo (1338m/4554ft) beside the Río Ara. Accommodation includes a refuge and a campsite.

Bujaruelo to Refugio Delgado Úbeda (de Gòriz)

Follow the road (or the footpath on the opposite bank) alongside the Río Ara downstream, to pass through the impressive Bujaruelo gorge onto the confluence with the Río Arazas in the Ordesa Valley. Now follow the route described in the first day of Trek 6 to Refugio Delgado Úbeda (de Gòriz).

Refugio Delgado Úbeda (de Gòriz) to Parador Turismo de 'Monte Perdido'

At first, take the route for the second day of Trek 6 until you reach the Collado de Añisclo. From here, a steep path descends to the road, which leads back to the starting point at the Parador Turismo de 'Monte Perdido' (1290m/4232ft).

TREK 8: ON THE PATH OF THE BEAR

Approaching from the west, this remote area between the two provinces of Aragón and Navarra is the true start of the alpine Pyrenees. From the plain of the Río Aragón Subordán, the mountains rise gently until they reach an elevation of 2662m (8734ft). Due to this natural rock barrier, the valleys situated on the southern side are protected against the bad weather that prevails from the north-west and have a fundamentally drier climate than areas further to the west in Navarra. These remote valleys are among the least populated in Spain.

TREK ESSENTIALS

LENGTH: 6 days.
ACCESS: Take the N330 from Huesca to Sabiñánigo and then the N240 to Jaca and Puente Jaca. After Puente Jaca take a right turn to Ansó and on to Zuriza.
DIFFICULTY: Moderate to strenuous.
HIGHEST POINT: Pico de Los Tres Reyes (2444m/8018ft).
TREK STYLE: Camping and refuges.
MAPS: Editorial Alpina 1:35 000 Belagua Ansó Echo (Miguel Angelo).
FURTHER OPTIONS: Climb Bisaurin (2670m/8760ft).

Zuriza to Refugio de Belagua

The first day of the trek is relatively easy and provides a good opportunity to get used to the weight of the rucksack. From the beautifully situated and excellent campsite in Zuriza (1227m/4026ft) head north on the partially asphalted track, following the course of the Barranco de Petrechema gently up through a wooded valley. Looking back, there are marvellous views of the Alanos mountain range in the distance. After 4km (2⅓ miles), the route passes by the Refugio de Linza (1400m/4593ft), which provides an excellent excuse to stop for cold drinks and a *bocadillo* (sandwich). From behind the hut, climb the wooded slope that heads north-west to the Collado Aztapenta (1545m/5069ft), which borders the two provinces of Navarra and Aragón.

Brown bears (*Ursus actos*), although rare, can still be found in the Aragones-Navarro Pyrenees.

From the col, descend into the Rincón de Belagua, at the bottom of which a good track can be picked up down to the main road between Izaba and France. Turn right at the road and follow it for about 800m (½ mile) to where a path goes off to the right. Follow the path up a steep slope until reaching the Refugio de Belagua (1428m/4685ft).

Refugio de Belagua to Refugio de Linza

Where others turn back the adventure is only just beginning, as today it is necessary to cross the karst labyrinth known as Larra. Leave the refuge as early as possible to allow time for the long and complicated route that lies ahead.

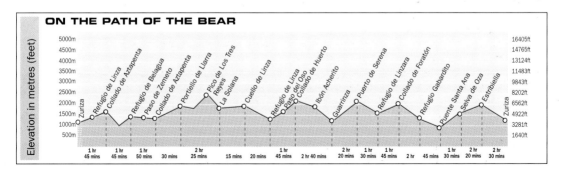

ON THE PATH OF THE BEAR

The alpine landscape in the valley of Aguas Tuertas is one of the most beautiful in the whole of the Pyrenees, both French and Spanish.

From the hut, return down the path towards the road. Just after the Paso de Zemeto, at a height of 1310m (4298ft), take a path off to the east and ascend through a little valley, staying north of Lapazarra peak until you reach the Lapazarra col. The terrain undulates for the next 3km (1¾ miles) before starting to ascend.

The way across the chaotic landscape of Larra (1770m/5807ft) is difficult to follow due to the complete lack of paths and rough terrain. However, occasional splashes of yellow paint and cairns do mark the way. The route eventually begins to ascend more steeply and finally reaches the Lhurs col. From here, traverse round to the right until you reach a saddle. To the left, an ascent leads to La Mesa de Los Tres Reyes (Table of the Three Kings). Legend has it that in the 12th century, at the top of this 2421-m (7943-ft) peak, which forms the convergence of France, Aragón and Navarra, the three kings of the aforementioned areas had a meeting, with each sitting in his own terrain. Today, a plaque on the summit commemorates the occasion. To the right is the Pico de los Tres Reyes (2444m/8018ft) and the main way on. An easy gully to the south of the summit gives access to the top from where there are marvellous views of the surrounding peaks – Pico Anie to the north, Peñablanca to the north-east and Petrechema and Acherito to the south.

Descend the western ridge to reach a small col. The way down is south-westwards, traversing diagonally across the hillside on grassy terrain with occasional rocky sections. After descending some 400m (1312ft) a more well-trodden path continues down in a westerly direction until it reaches La Solana, a depression where cattle and horses graze during the summer months. From here, follow a visible path to the Cuello de Linza, where there is a spring with lovely fresh water. From the *cuello*, descend through alpine pastures and meadows, which are adorned with numerous colourful orchids during the spring, to the Refugio de Linza, your accommodation for the night. For those who have any energy left, it is worth taking a stroll in the fading light to try and spot some local wildlife, such as deer or tawny owls.

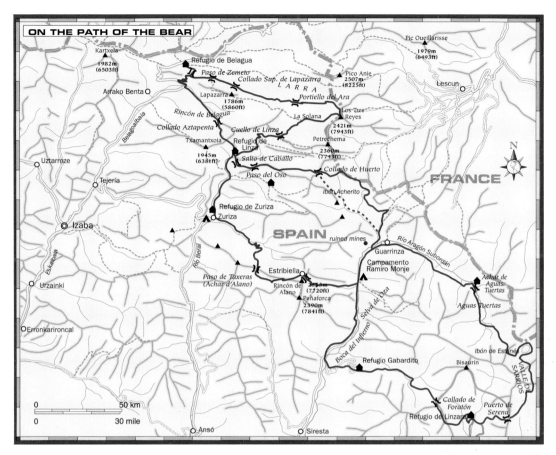

Refugio de Linza to Campamento Ramiro Monje

Cross the river in front of the refuge and turn towards the striking crevice of Salto de Caballo (1400m/4593ft). Follow the crevice up though beech forest on a steep and muddy path. On reaching the top of this short climb, turn left (east) and continue up the slope ahead. You will soon reach the Paso del Oso (1640m/5381ft), the so-called 'Bears' Path'. Here, situated between the French Pyrenees and the valleys of Belagua and Anso, a few examples of the shy Brown bear still survive. Unfortunately (or perhaps fortunately), the chances of seeing one of these impressive creatures face to face is extremely unlikely.

From the Paso del Oso, the route turns left and enters a marvellous and spacious valley, the Plana de Diego, at the end of which and slightly over to the right is the Collado de Huerto (2153m/7064ft).

On crossing the col, with its fantastic views over the valley of the Río Aragón Subordán, there are two options. One option is to drop down to the river below and follow it on a well-trodden path down to the car-park at Guarrinza. The other, more

interesting alternative is to traverse the hillside in an easterly direction, trying not to lose height until reaching the Ibón Acherito (1875m/6152ft). From the lake there are marvellous views of the Gamutea, Mallo de Acherito and Petrachema peaks; the latter's rocky pinnacles frequently attract the attention of ambitious rock climbers. From the lake follow the obvious path down to Guarrinza, where there are some deserted buildings of a former mine and an old police station dating back to the Spanish Civil War. A further 3km (1¾ miles) down the track, heading south, is a campsite, Campamento Ramiro Monje.

Campamento Ramiro Monje to Refugio de Linzara

Follow the track back upstream alongside the Río Aragón Subordán through a lush, green and spacious valley to Achar de Aguas Tuertas, with its fine waterfall, El Salto, which is passed after climbing a zigzagging path on the right. The trek now enters the enchanting hanging valley of Aguas Tuertas, with the clear waters of the Río Aragón Subordán slowly meandering through it. As chamoix graze in this high alpine pasture, marmots can be heard

From the karst labyrinths of La Larra, famous for its deep cave systems, rise the peaks of Anialarra, Los Tres Reyes and Petrechema.

whistling loudly, warning each other of the presence of man or perhaps even of a golden eagle hunting for sustenance. All such activity will be observed by the ever-watchful eye of one of the rare and endangered lammergeier vultures that rove the skies above the valley.

Follow the valley until you reach Ibón de Estanés (1777m/5830ft) at the valley's end. This lovely lake, surrounded by mountains, provides the perfect spot for a well-earned rest.

Circumnavigate the lake on the left-hand side and then turn south into the hanging valley of Los Sarrios, which is marked with cairns. Ahead lies the steep and arduous ascent to the spacious Puerto de Serena (2200m/7218ft), from where you descend into the valley, past some huts in Los Puertos, which separates the massifs of Bisaurin and Bernera. The clear path now leads along the south-east flank of the Bisaurin massif down to the Refugio de Linzara (1540m/5052ft) situated at the foot of this mountain.

Refugio de Linzara to Campamento Ramiro Monje
Leave the refuge and climb westwards to the Collado de Poratón (2032m/6667ft), from where the route leads directly over alpine pastures down to the Refugio Gabardito (1400m/4593ft). At the refuge, which is open all year and lies protected in the shade of a pine forest, provisions can be replenished.

BIRDS OF PREY

The wild gorges and endless woods of the remote area between the provinces of Aragón and Navarra are home to almost all of the birds of prey resident in southern Europe. By far the most common is the griffon vulture (*Gyps fulvus*) (pictured) with its gigantic wings, which can be seen frequently soaring high above the peaks or along the ridges searching for thermals. The strikingly coloured Egyptian vulture (*Neophron percnopterus*) often frequents the outskirts of villages and is in constant competition with elegant red and black kites (*Milvus milvus* and *Milvus migrans*) in their search for sustenance.

In contrast, the lammergeier vulture (*Gypaëtus barbatus*) lives in complete isolation amongst the unapproachable and colossal rock faces that rise majestically from the valleys. Lonely, he prowls through his gargantuan territory, looking for the cadavers that other scavengers have left behind. The only places where lammergeiers are regularly seen face to face are at the dedicated feeding places that have been established within the last few years, where farmers donate dead cattle, sheep or horses and other carcasses to feed these incredible animals.

The secluded gorges are also home to a variety of interesting smaller birds, such as the wheatear (*Oenanthe oenanthe*) and the elegant alpine swift (*Apus melba*).

PEAK: BISAURIN

CLIMB ESSENTIALS

SUMMIT Bisaurin 2670m (8758ft).
CAMP Refugio de Linzara.
GRADE Scramble Grade 1.

Using Refugio de Linzara as a base, Bisaurin – the highest peak in the Spanish western Pyrenees – is easily climbed in a day; the simplest route is via the south ridge.

Leave the refuge and climb the grassy slope to the north-west, which leads to the Collado de Poratón (2030m/6660ft). From the col, climb an arduous 650m (2133ft) up a steep rocky slope with sections of scree to the summit and a breathtaking panorama. The views stretch into the horizon across Aragon and a large part of the western Pyrenees.

Descent is either by reversing the route, or by descending the peak's south-eastern flank and then following the ridge of Las Fetas down to approximately 2200m (7220ft), where you turn west and drop into the El Puerto valley and back down to the refuge.

The simplest way of ascending Bisaurin is by scrambling up the south ridge.

Descend into the valley of the Río Aragón Subordán on an asphalt road; alternatively, take the path that descends between the switchbacks in the road. Once at the valley bottom cross the river on a bridge. On reaching the main road a signpost (Camino Antiguo) marks the start of an old Roman path that goes to Selva de Oza after passing through the impressively narrow Boca del Infierno (Hell's Abyss). Head for Campamento Ramiro Monje, as before.

Campamento Ramiro Monje to Zuriza

From the campsite, return down the road and, after crossing a bridge over the Río Aragón Subordán for the last time, you will spot a forestry hut on the edge of a clearing. From behind this hut, an obvious path enters the forest. The path climbs in zigzags above the Barranco de Estribiella, past a spectacular waterfall and then along the Cuenca Herbosa, where there are views of the east face of the dominating Peñaforca in front. Soon the path goes off to the right and rises through a little gully below Rincón de Alano to the Estribiella pass (2006m/6581ft). In a westerly direction rise the towering buttresses of the Alanos range, with Ezkaurre protruding in the distance. To the north Petrechema and Pico Anie loom up above the landscape, whereas if you look back in an easterly direction there is a fantastic panorama of the whole Río Aragón Subordán and Selva de Oza.

Fulfilled by marvellous impressions throughout the day, and with the afternoon sun casting long shadows over the landscape, walk over the gentle meadows in the direction of Paso de Taxeras (Achar d'Alano) (1260m/4134ft), where a good track is joined. The final section back to the starting point of Zuriza is in the shade of a beech forest that harbours the rare white-backed woodpecker.

TREK 9: RONCESVALLES AND ALTO IRATI

Navarra is, along with the independent autonomous provinces of the Pais Vasco and La Rioja, one of the smallest provinces in Spain and is typified in its north by sleepy mountain villages surrounded by immense woodlands, part-natural, part-cultivated. The foothills of this, the western extremity of the Pyrenees, rise gently to over 1500m (4921ft) in height and, because of the humid climate, consist of extensive dense forests through which run clear rivers and streams. Autumn is the most delightful season in which to visit as the beech forests take on a new range of golden colours.

TREK ESSENTIALS

LENGTH: 6 days; 147.75km (88½ miles).
ACCESS: From Pamplona, take the N135 north to Roncesvalles.
DIFFICULTY: Moderate.
HIGHEST POINT: Ezkaurre 2049m (6722ft).
TREK STYLE: Refuges and hotels.
MAPS: Editorial Alpina 1:25 000 Roncesvalles, Selva de Irati, Ori and 1:35 000 Belagua Ansó Echo (Miguel Angelo).
FURTHER OPTIONS: Ascent of Pico Ori.

Ermita de San Salvador to Albergue Mendilatz

Start from the small chapel of Ermita de San Salvador (1062m/3484ft) directly on the Roncesvalles–France road. Heading east, follow a marked track, known as Napoleon's Way, up a hillside. After passing the little Igalepo peak (1282m/4206ft) you will soon arrive at Collado Lepoeder (1445m/4741ft). From the col the way forks and turns left across the pass in a north-easterly direction. If you don't mind a short diversion, to the right a 2-km (⅓-mile) hike up the track leads to the radio transmitter on top of Ortzanzurieta (1570m/5148ft), from where there are marvellous views over the Irati area and parts of the upper Navarra in the Pyrenean foothills.

The main trek, however, heads across a flat area from the col. Soon Napoleon's Way veers off to the left, but the trek stays on the main track to

A damp climate ensures that the plentiful streams and rivers roar through the dense woodlands all the year round.

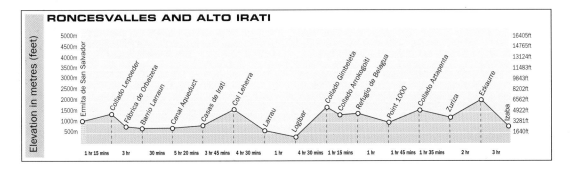

RONCESVALLES AND ALTO IRATI

The impressive Los Alanos range dominates Zuriza in the Upper Anso valley.

follow the GR11 eastwards. On joining the Barranco Etxasakese in a beech valley, head down until you reach an old disused smelting works and arms factory, Fábrica de Orbaizeta (850m/2800ft), left over from the Spanish Civil War (1936–39). From the deserted factory it is only a few hundred metres to the village of Barrio Larraun (approx. 700m/2300ft) and the Albergue Mendilatz.

Albergue Mendilatz to Casa de Irati (del Rey)

Leave the small Pyrenean village of Barrio Larraun and follow the narrow road in the direction of Orbaizeta. After about 2km (1⅓ miles), where an aqueduct crosses the road, take the small path that branches off to the left and you will soon reach the Río Irati. Just before the bridge turn towards the east and follow the river upstream. This enchanting riverside path immediately leads deeper into dense forest along the Río Irati. This quiet beech and pine wood is the hunting ground for dippers and, if one treads quietly, it's not uncommon to hear the call of black woodpeckers. In this natural self-seeding forest countless fallen tree trunks of stately size sometimes inhibit the way on.

After following the river for about 2 hours the path leads to the northern side of the Embalse de

Irabia (820m/2690ft) dam. From here, the route goes round the lake to the forestry hut, Casa Berzal, on the northern side of the Río Irati. The final destination for the night, Casa de Irati (del Rey), is reached by following the GR11/12.

ROLAND'S SONG

The Roncesvalles area became well known over 1,200 years ago due to a famous episode chronicled in history. The event took place near the Ibañeta pass that joins Spain to France during the withdrawal of Charlemagne's Spanish campaign against the Moors in 778.

Charlemagne's rear-guard was attacked by the Basques, and Roland, the campaign commander, too proud to summon for help by blowing his horn, was duly slain. According to legend, to honour the commander *La Chanson de Roland*, 'Roland's song', was written as an accolade to his bravery. During the Middle Ages, troubadours (travelling singers) would recount the story across southern Europe.

However, this account of events is almost complete fiction. The 11th-century epic poem, or *chanson de geste*, is essentially a compilation of other written and oral histories – most of which themselves appeared for the first time 300 years after the battle.

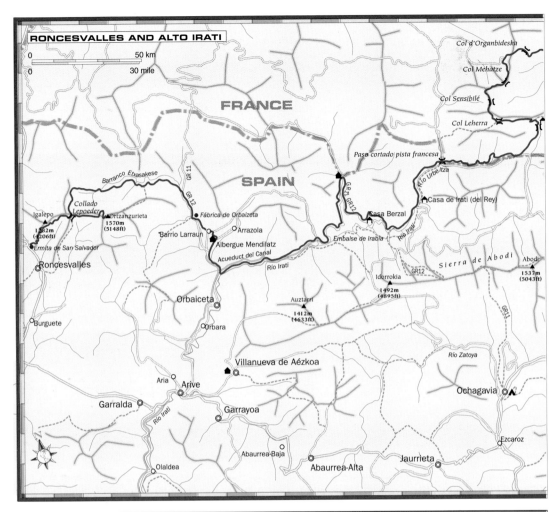

RONCESVALLES AND ALTO IRATI

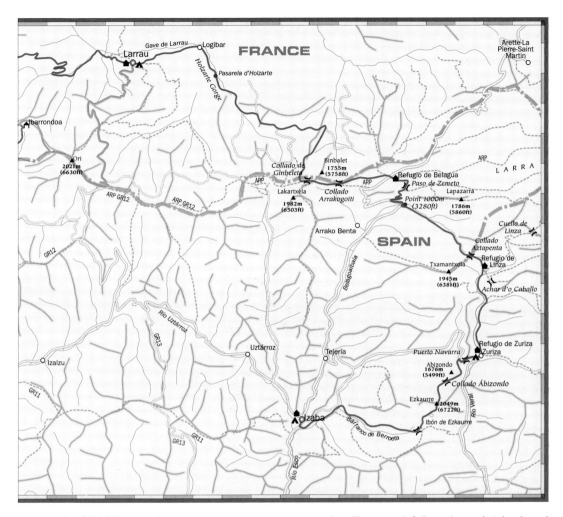

Casa de Irati (del Rey) to Larrau

If climbing Pico Ori it's wise to leave Casa de Irati as early as possible, as a long and exhausting day lies in front. Follow the Río Urbeltza north along the track. After approximately ½ hour, on reaching a small bridge (895m/2936ft), cross over and turn immediately left to follow the valley up towards the east. You now cross into French territory and gain height through marvellous woods. After reaching a small pass, the valley opens and there is a hut, Ibarrondoa (1300m/4265ft), on the right-hand side. From here, the track is followed directly down to the French mountain village of Larrau (650m/2133ft), where you can stay in the hotel, refuge or campsite.

Larrau to Refugio de Belagua

Again, set out as early as possible. Leave the

As evening draws in the moon slowly emerges above the rock face of the Veral gorge near Zuriza.

mountain village and follow the quiet backroad some 2km (1⅓ miles) downhill towards Logibar until you reach an *albergue*. The trek now diverts south (GR10) and climbs parallel to the Holzarte Gorge. Cross the gorge on its spectacular suspension bridge, the Pasarela d'Holzarte, which hangs some 150m (500ft) above the river. Ascend through woodland to the head of the gorge, known as Ohadibia Zubia and head south on a series of zigzags up the steep hillside until you join a jeep track. Follow the track for some 6km (3⅔ miles), until you reach a zigzagging path to the right that goes up to the Collado de Ginbeleta, which marks the border with Spain (1677m/5502ft).

From the col, the route heads east along the ARP (Alto Ruta Pirenieca/High Pyrenean Route), bypassing Binbalet peak on the right and descending to the Collado Arrakogoiti (1418m/4652ft). Finally, traverse along the hillside without losing height to the Refugio de Belagua (1428m/4685ft).

PEAK: PICO ORI

CLIMB ESSENTIALS

SUMMIT: Pico Ori 2021m (6631ft).
CAMP: Ibarrondoa hut.
GRADE: Scramble Grade 3.

From the Ibarrondoa hut turn right (south-east) up the north-western slope of Zaspigaña peak. From here it's necessary to cross, or circumnavigate, the delicate and steep Brecha de Alupiña on a vertiginous section. Care is required as a certain amount of scrambling is involved.

Throughout the winter and long into the summer months, the northern side of the *brecha* contains frozen snow, which makes passage almost impossible to those without suitable equipment and experience. From the southern side of the *brecha* follow the ridge to the summit.

The way down is via what is considered to be the 'normal' route up. Descend via the scree slope on the southern side of the south-east ridge, skirting below the sub-peak of Ori Txipia to join the main road at Puerto de Larrau. From here, follow the road north for about 2km (1⅓ miles) to Col d'Erroimendi and then down into the town of Larrau.

Pico Ori is an attractive and fairly easy mountain to scale when you're in the area.

Refugio de Belagua to Zuriza

Reverse the first day of Trek 8 (see page 73).

Zuriza to Izaba

Leave Zuriza (1200m/3937ft) heading west and after approximately 1km (⅔ mile) you will reach a junction. Take a sharp right and follow the road for 1.5km (1 mile) to reach a small col, Puerto Navarra (1290m/4232ft). Turn left (south) and follow a vague path into a sparse wood. Circumnavigate the base of Abizondo peak on its left-hand side. When you reach a small valley, a path ascends to the Collado Abizondo (1638m/5374ft) on the north flank of Ezkaurre. Continue to follow the small valley up until you reach another pass at 1638m (5374ft). Turn left and climb the remaining 400m (1300ft) to Ezkaurre's summit (2049m/6722ft), using a kind of gully in places over rock.

Although the ascent presents no real difficulties, it's not advisable to attempt this route in bad weather. From the summit, there are marvellous panoramas of the adjacent mountains, including the spectacular walls of Alanos, Los Tres Reyes and Pico Anie. From the top, a vague path leads down to Ibón de Ezkaurre, from where you follow the ridge a short distance south-west to a col. Descend the slope to the west and you will soon pick up a jeep track, which you follow down to Izaba. In this charming medieval mountain village there is a hotel, a refuge, a campsite and several *casas rurales*.

To return to Roncesvalles, either take a taxi or embark on a 3-day hike along the GR11.

WESTERN (ARAGONES-NAVARRO) PYRENEES DIRECTORY

GETTING THERE

By air: Barcelona and Bilbao are the most convenient airports for the Western and Navarro-Aragones Pyrenees. These airports are served by many different airlines including British Airways, BMI British Midland and Iberia. The high season for tickets is July and August, Easter and Christmas. If you're booking quite far in advance, look out for cheap deals on Easy Jet and Go.
BMI (British Midland): www.britishmidlands.com
British Airways: www.britishairways.com
Easy Jet: www.easyjet.com
Go Airlines: www.go-fly.com
Iberia Airlines: www.iberia.com

By train: Train services run to and from Sabiñániago and Jaca, the main access points for the Western and Navarro-Aragones Pyrenees. To confirm train times, contact:
Bilbao Train Station: C/Gurtubay 1; tel. 944 395077
Bilbao Termíbus station: tel. 944 395205
Huesca Train Station: Av. de Zaragoza; tel. 974 242159
Jaca Train Station: C/Ferrocarriles; tel. 974 361332
Pamplona Train Station: Avda San Jorge; tel. 948 130202/948 227282
RENFE, Barcelona: tel. 93 4900202

By bus: There is a regular service to Sabiñániago from Huesca and Jaca. To confirm bus times, contact:
Bilbao Bus Station: Calle Hurtado de Amezaga; tel. 944 238623
Bilbao Termíbus station: tel. 944 395205
Huesca Bus Station: Av. del Parque s/n; tel. 9742 210700
Jaca Bus Station: Avda Jacetania; tel. 974 355060
Pamplona Bus Station: C/Conde Oliveto 8; tel. 948 223854

ACCOMMODATION

Refuge Information: www.refugiosyalbergues.com

Manned Refuges

Albergue de Añisclo (1280m/4200ft): 36 places; open all year; tel. 974 489010; fax 974 489008
Albergue de Casa Iriarte (750m/2461ft): 51 places; open all summer and on weekends in winter; tel. 948 890070
Albergue de Roncesvalles: 58 places; open all year; tel. 948 760302/948 760364
Logibar Larrau (380m/1247ft): 15 places; open all year; tel. 05 928 6114 (France)
Refugio de Belagua (Club Deportivo Navarra) (1428m/4685ft): tel. 948 394002/974 373291/974 373222
Refugio Bujaruelo (Río Ara) (1338m/4390ft): 24 places; open in summer; tel. 974 486428

Refugio de Gabardito (Hecho) (1380m/4528ft): 36 places; open all year; tel. 974 375387
Refugio de Gòriz (2195m/7202ft): 96 places; open all year; tel. 974 341201
Refugio Herriberri (923m/3028ft): 30 places; open all year
Refugio Irabia (975m/3199ft): 5 places; free
Refugio Irati (1327m/4354ft): 24 places; open all year; tel. 05 928 5129 (France)
Refugio de Linza (Anso) (1350m/4429ft): Open all year; tel. 974 370112/974 375176/974 375048
Refugio de Linzarra: (currently uninhabitable)
Refugio/Albergue Lucien Briet: tel. 974 486221
Refugio Mendilatz: 45 places; restaurant; tel. 948 766088
Refugio Otsagbia: Calle Mayor, 8; tel. 948 890070
Refugio de Pineta (1220m/4003ft): 71 places; open all year; tel. 974 341147/974 501203
Refugio Ronariza or Refugio Ordiso (Valle de Ara) (1800m/5906ft): 10 places; free
Refuge des Sarradets (Refuge de Brèche Roland) (2587m/8488ft): 85 places; fax 05 629 24041 (France)
Refugio Tucarroya (2661m/8731ft): 15 places; free.
Refugio Zuriza (camping) (1227m/4026ft): 64 places; open all year; tel. 974 370196

TOURIST INFORMATION

Navarra Tourist Office: Calle Duque de Ahumada 3, Pamplona; tel. 941 340300/948 220741

Anso: tel. 974 370082
Bilbao: Teatro Arriga; tel. 944 795760
Hecho: tel. 974 375026/974 375329
Huesca: C/General Lasheras; tel. 974 225778/974 292100
Izaba: tel. 948 893251
Jaca: Avda Regimiento de Galicia; tel. 974 360098
Larrau (F): tel. 0033 559 28 61 29
Otsagabia: tel. 948 890004
Puente La Reina: tel. 974 377201 (summer only)
Roncal: tel. 948 475136
Roncesvalles: C/Ant. Molino; tel. 948 760193
Sabiñániago: tel. 974 480055
Torla: tel. 974 486152/974 229804
Torla Park Information: tel. 974 486212

EMERGENCY NUMBERS

S.O.S.: tel. 112
Mountain Rescue: tel. 05 629 24824 (France)
Guardia Civil: tel. 062
Hospital Jaca (emergency): tel. 974 363772

6

CORDILLERA CANTÁBRICA

Treks in the Cordillera Cantábrica take you through land-scapes that have captured the imagination of mountaineers and nature lovers for centuries. Deep limestone ravines wind their way through lush forests, while above tower absurd and amazing rock formations.

Due to the natural barriers between the Basque country to the east and Asturias to the west, the people of Cantabria have developed a distinct and long-lived culture from that of their neighbours.

The Río Ebro thunders through a dramatic gorge near Pesquera de Ebro (trek 10).

On the southern side of the impressive Cordillera Cantábrica the culture, as well as the landscape, changes abruptly. The geology of the region, which is fundamentally older than the nearby precipitous Picos de Europa, consists mainly of conglomerate as opposed to limestone. The barren ridges overgrown with broom bushes are almost impenetrable. Due to deforestation, dense forests are rare and because of the hard and impermeable nature of the surface, numerous streams and rivers are to be found everywhere. The Fuentes Carrionas National Park, considered the apex of the Cordillera Cantábrica, borders the areas between the provinces of Cantabria, León and Palencia. Here, the highest peaks of this range, Peña Prieta (2539m/8330ft), Curavacas (2524m/8281ft) and Espigüete (2451m/8042ft) dominate the surrounding countryside. Espigüete stands out in particular due to its distinct character – unlike the surrounding mountains, this colossal peak is composed of limestone, which gives it an almost shiny appearance.

The central zone of the national park is one of the most remote areas of the Cordillera with only a few shepherds living here during the summer months. The southern flanks stretch out gently to join the northern plains of the Meseta, and the whole area, characterized by its extreme continental climate, is subject to hot dry summers and extremely cold snowy winters not dissimilar to that of Alaska.

The source of the Río Carrion is to be found among these dark and forbidding peaks.

Local Flora and Fauna

As mentioned above, the valleys and slopes of the Fuentes Carrionas National Park have been cleared of woodland to create grazing land for cattle, horses and sheep. Nevertheless, some woods still exist, made up of small oaks on the warmer southern slopes along with beech and birch that continue to survive on the more exposed positions.

Increasingly over the last few years there have been important pine and spruce plantations established, which stand out like patchwork quilts due to the surrounding firebreaks. The largest part of the area is, however, overgrown with thickets of broom and heather.

During the summer months, the meadows and alpine pastures are host to a number of interesting and remarkable plants, with different species of gentians, orchids, narcissi and lilies flowering in abundance.

Heart-flowered Serapias (*Serapias cordigera*) is a member of the orchid family and flowers between March and May.

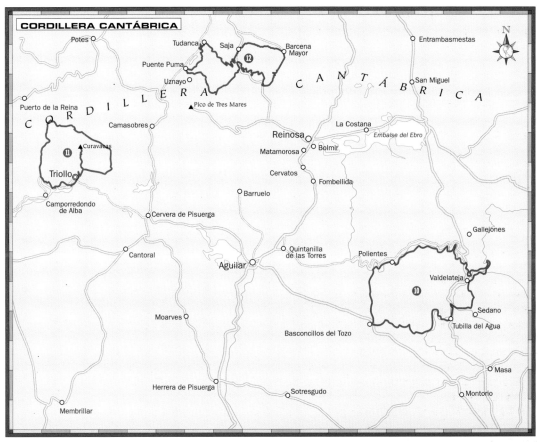

The fauna found here is by no means of less importance. In the bird world highlights such as the Golden and Booted Eagle exist, along with some unusual songbirds, including the Rock thrush, Ring ouzel, and a small colony of Bluethroats that live around the boggy headwaters of the Río Carrion.

These staunch peaks and valleys are also one of the last retreats in Spain for the Cantabrian Brown bear and Iberian wolf and fortunately, due to widespread protection, their numbers are on the increase. Far more common to watch, however, are red deer and chamoix, which populate the hillside, along with Roe deer, foxes, badgers and martens.

The marvellously clear waters that flow through the upper reaches of the valleys are the natural habitat for numerous otters that feed off an abundance of trout.

The church bell is still in place in the near-deserted village of Cardaño de Arriba.

TREK 10: THE RAVINES OF THE ALTO EBRO AND RÍO RUDRÓN

South-east of the Picos de Europa, in the southern tip of Cantabria where the mountains of the Cordillera Cantábrica slowly turn into the plateau of the northern Meseta, the Río Ebro flows. This river, one of the longest in Spain, gives its name not only to the surrounding countryside but to the whole peninsula ('Ebro' comes from the Roman word 'Iber', hence Iberia). Here, to the north of Burgos, the young Ebro and its tributaries, such as the Río Rudrón, have carved gigantic gorges into the karst landscape of the Meseta. Along the rivers are marvellous quiet tracks linking sleepy medieval villages.

TREK ESSENTIALS

LENGTH: 5 days; 93km (55½ miles).
ACCESS: From Santander, take the motorway to Torrelavega and then in the direction of Bilbao. After passing through Vargas take the main road (N623) south in the direction of Burgos. In the village of Escalada, turn right and follow the road along the Río Ebro to Polientes.
DIFFICULTY: Easy.
TREK STYLE: Small hotels; book in advance.
HIGHEST POINT: 1090m (3576ft).
MAPS: Mapa Guia 1:200 000 Cordillera Cantábrica.
FURTHER OPTIONS: None.

Many of the houses are adorned with splendid *esqudos*, traditional family coats of arms. An unusual feature of this area is the prevalence of small chapels carved out of the rock faces. These, along with many deserted villages, are remnants of a time gone by when this picturesque area of Spain was more densely populated.

The gorges and limestone plateaux are particularly interesting for bird and plant lovers. Without doubt, May is the best time for a visit as many splendid orchids flourish across the countryside, and the fledglings of many raptors will have

hatched so their parents will be hunting constantly in an attempt to tame the perpetual hunger of their young.

Polientes to Orbaneja del Castillo

On the banks of the Río Ebro sits the small village of Polientes (760m/2493ft), the capital of the Valderredible valley, where accommodation and provisions are easily found.

At the eastern end of the village turn right, cross over the river and then turn left onto a track, which after 1km (⅗ mile) becomes a path. Follow the path over meadows and pastures and through marvellous woodlands until you reach the little village of San Martin de Elines. The village's impressive 10th-century Colegiata de Elines is perhaps one of the most important collegiate churches in Cantabria. It was once used for the instruction of monks and there have been various archaeological discoveries made on the site.

From here, walk along the riverside to Villaescusa de Ebro (700m/2297ft). Continue along the small path that follows the river. With a bit of luck you may spot one of the numerous woodpeckers that hide in the shady woods, or even the beautiful golden oriole. Gradually the gorge narrows and after about 3–3½ hours some strange rock formations come into view opposite the

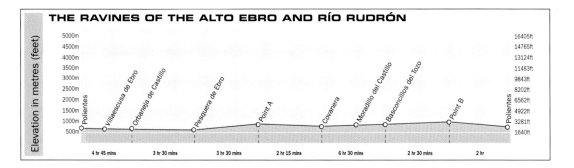

THE RAVINES OF THE ALTO EBRO AND RÍO RUDRÓN

Near Pesquera de Ebro the steep rock face of this spectacular ravine rises some 200m (650ft) from the Río Ebro, providing a perfect breeding ground for birds of prey.

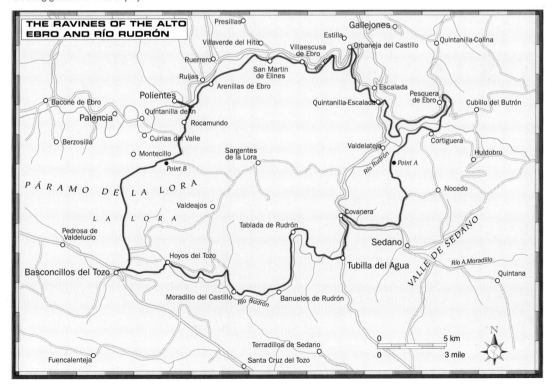

THE RAVINES OF THE ALTO EBRO AND RÍO RUDRÓN

Presillas
Gallejones
Estilla
Quintanilla-Colina
Villaverde del Hito
Villaescusa de Ebro
Orbaneja del Castillo
Ruerrero
San Martin de Elines
Ruijas
Arenillas de Ebro
Escalada
Pesquera de Ebro
Cubillo del Butrón
Polientes
Quintanilla-Escalada
Bacone de Ebro
Quintanilla de An
Palencia
Rocamundo
Berzosilla
Cuirlas del Valle
Valdelateja
Cortiguera
Huidobro
Montecillo
Sargentes de la Lora
Point A
Río Rudrón
Point B
PÁRAMO DE LA LORA
Nocedo
Valdeajos
LA LORA
Tablada de Rudrón
Covanera
Pedrosa de Valdelucio
Sedano
VALLE DE SEDANO
Hoyos del Tozo
Tubilla del Agua
Río A.Moradillo
Basconcillos del Tozo
Quintana
Moradillo del Castillo
Río Rudrón
Banuelos de Rudrón
Terradillos de Sedano
Fuencalenteja
Santa Cruz del Tozo

0   5 km
0   3 mile

N

A family coat of arms (*esqudo*) adorns the front of an old ruined palace in Cortiguera.

village of Orbaneja del Castillo. Cross the river on a footbridge and ascend to the village perched on rocks way above the river. Due to a recent increase in tourism, it's now possible to find accommodation and food in this picturesque village.

Orbaneja del Castillo to Pesquera de Ebro

Return back down to the river and cross the footbridge. Turn right and continue along the banks of the Río Ebro. After approximately 1 hour following this scenic river, the route passes by the villages of Escalada and Quintanilla-Escalada. Cross the Río Ebro once again on the bridge beside the Santander–Burgos main road and turn right to follow the left-hand bank of the river. The trek soon takes you past a small chapel, La Ermita de Nuestra Señora de Ebro.

Directly behind the nearby hydroelectric power station, take a narrow path to go through one of the most secluded parts of this mini 'Grand Canyon of Spain'. This section of the trek is

---

FLORA AND FAUNA OF THE MESETA

The rough northern Meseta – a plateau that stretches from south of the Cordillera Cantábrica over most of central Spain – has a continental climate marked by cold rainy winters and dry hot summers. The average height of the region ranges from 800m (2600ft) in the valleys, to approximately 1000m (3280ft) on the plains. On the high plateau, which during winter is subject to icy storms, broom (*Cytisus scoparius*), juniper (*Juniperus*) and small holm oak (*Quercus ilex*) prosper. An impressive number of orchids (*Dactylorhiza*) (pictured below) grow alongside other flowers, such as gladioli (*Gladiolus*) and hyacinths (*Muscari*).

In the valley bottoms and along the brooks you will find alder (*Alnus glutinosa*), willow (*Salix*) and poplar trees (*Populus*), while extensive oak

(*Quercus*) with mixed deciduous and coniferous trees grow along the steep sides of the gorges.

The bird life is no less interesting, particularly the birds of prey in this area. The rock faces that form the impressive gorges are home to many vulture colonies, including the Egyptian vulture (*Neophron percnopterus*). Also to be found here are eagles, such as Golden (*Aquila chrysaetos*), Booted (*Hieraaetus pennatus*), Short-toed (*Ciraetus gallicus*) and an important population of the rare Bonelli's eagle (*Hieraaetus fasciatus*). In addition, little bustards (*Tetrax tetrax*) live in the surrounding area of the Paramo de la Lora.

In the mammal kingdom the wolf (*Canis lupus*) (pictured above) is perhaps the most striking local species and, over the last few years, reports of sightings have occurred more frequently along the valleys of the Upper Ebro. Furthermore, living in the dense woods of this hilly landscape, is an exceptionally large population of Roe deer (*Capreolus capreolus*) and in the meandering brooks and rivers a healthy number of otter (*Lutra lutra*), trout (*Salmo trutta*) and eels (*Anguilla anguilla*).

Abstract rock formations, such as these found near Orbaneja de Castillo, are characteristic of the ravines of the Ebro valley.

particularly interesting for ornithologists and nature-lovers, because here can be seen a variety of birds, such as kingfishers, dippers, Peregrine falcons and the majestic golden eagle. The walls of the canyon soon diminish as the path leaves the river to enter the medieval village of Pesquera de Ebro (680m/2231ft). In this village, which was founded in the 9th century by King Alfonso III, are some remarkable *esqudos*; accommodation can be found in the hotel or campsite.

Pesquera de Ebro to Covanera

After passing the old village church, return back to the Río Ebro along the road and cross the river on a bridge that dates back to the Middle Ages. Follow the road for some hundred metres and then turn right onto a small path above the river that leads to the ghost village of Cortiguera after approximately 1 hour. From the village follow the ravine in a south-westerly direction, with fine views of the grand Ebro canyon which has been etched out of the surrounding plateau. If the weather is clear, it's possible to see the snow-covered peaks of the Alto Campoo ski resort on the horizon to the north-east.

The path gradually ascends in a southerly direction to reach a high point in an area called La Lora (about 1000m/3280ft) and after 2–3 hours joins a backroad that descends into the Moradillo valley. On reaching a crossroads, take the road to Covanera. Unfortunately, as no route exists along the river at this point, it's necessary to walk the last 3–4km (2–3 miles) along the road to Covanera (approximately 700m/2297ft). In Covanera, situated at the confluence of the rivers Moradillo and Rudrón, there is the possibility of staying the night in a *casa rurale*. During the evening it's worth making an excursion to the nearby Pozo Azul, a well-known cave that is completely flooded with water.

Covanera to Basconcillos del Tozo

Leave the village following the Río Rudrón in a southerly direction and after about 20 minutes go through Tubilla del Agua, perched high above the river. The route now turns to the west and

The gentle evening light adds contrast to the scenery around Hoyos del Tozo.

continues to follow the river as it meanders lazily through the hilly countryside. After a short time the path joins a small backroad that is followed up the romantic Rudrón Valley. Precipitous rock faces rise repeatedly from the steep slopes, and eagles and vultures soar the thermals.

After passing through several small villages the route takes you through Moradillo del Castillo (approx. 900m/2953ft), located on a rocky outcrop that seems to float above the river. Cross the village on the main road, which soon turns into a track, and 200m (220yd) after passing an old mill you will reach a junction – turn left and continue up the broad Río Rudrón. Soon the gorge becomes increasingly narrow and forested. This section of the trek is almost devoid of human presence. Only a few nature-lovers venture into this forest, so it's no surprise that it's not always easy to follow the narrow path. Towards the end of this section, where the rock faces are at their highest, numerous vultures, ravens and falcons breed.

After entering the small of village of Hoyos del Tozo, which has been built among colossal rocks,

cross a small bridge in the middle of the village and turn left in a southerly direction. The route now leaves the Rudrón valley on a wide track across fields and after about 45 minutes arrives at Basconcillos del Tozo (approx 1000m/3280ft) where you can stay in the local hotel.

Basconcillos del Tozo to Polientes

Set out from Basconcillos del Tozo in a northerly direction and follow the small road that heads towards Sargentes de la Lora. After about 2km (1¼ miles), where the road bends to the right, follow the track that goes straight on in a northerly direction across an inhospitable plateau inhabited by only a few animals and plants that have adapted to the extreme conditions. After following the track for about 2 hours a quiet backroad descends in switchbacks from the Páramo de la Lora back down to the Río Ebro. From the river there are marvellous views across the whole catchment area of the Upper Ebro. A small road descends into the valley and back to the starting point of Polientes.

TREK 11: THE ALASKA OF SPAIN

This remote area of the Cordillera Cantábrica lies south of the Picos de Europa and is often known as the roof of the Cordillera. Its wide open valleys tempt walkers and trekkers alike, while its gigantic mountains attract the rock-climbing faternity, all of whom will be unable to ignore the diverse flora and fauna of this unique alpine landscape.

TREK ESSENTIALS

LENGTH: 3–5 days; 41.25km (24¾ miles).
ACCESS: From the north, this area is of best reached on the N611 from Santander to Aguilar de Campoo. From Aguilar turn west on the P212 to Cevera de Pisuerga, and then continue on the P210 on the Ruta de los Pantanos to Triollo.
DIFFICULTY: Moderate (strenuous if peaks are climbed).
HIGHEST POINT: Saddle 2399m (7871ft).
TREK STYLE: Camping.
MAPS: Mapa Guia 1:50 000 Montaña Palentina.
FURTHER OPTIONS: Climb Espigüete, Peña Prieta and Curavacas.
RESTRICTIONS: It's worth asking for permission from one of the park rangers in Triollo before setting off; ask in the hotel.

The starting point of this trek is the small remote mountain village of Triollo (1298m/4258ft), situated next to the upper reservoir of the Río Carríon, the Embalse de Camporredondo de Alba.

Triollo to Refugio Espigüete

Leave Triollo on the road that goes south following the banks of the reservoir. After some hundred metres a track turns off to the right, leaving the colossal Curavacas peak behind. Trek across fields on the southern slopes of Peña Mario with streaming brooks cascading down the hillside to feed the glistening waters of the reservoir below. After about 1 hour the track rejoins the road just

The impressive north face of Curavacas with the 'Chalet Pedro' in the foreground.

THE ALASKA OF SPAIN

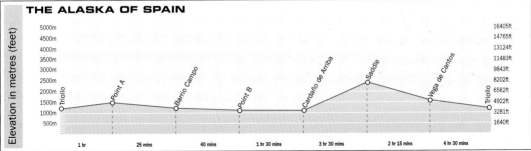

before entering the village of Barrio Campo, where a small colony of white storks nest on the banks of the reservoir. From here, another track again traverses the hillside, with red-backed shrike hiding in the hedgerows, along with red-legged partridge, quail, buzzards and red kites; during the winter months, the Great Grey shrike also populates these hills.

On the northernmost tip of the reservoir, a track heads off north immediately before the bridge that crosses the Arroyo de las Lomas. Take this path and follow it easily for about 2km (1¼ miles) until it's necessary to cross the river on a little bridge.

Join the road for the last section to the summer village of Cardaño de Arriba (1420m/4659ft), which is reputedly one of the highest villages in Spain. Just before the bridge (do not cross) that gains access to the village, a small track heading

north follows the riverside up to Refugio Espigüete where a camp can be set up for the night.

Refugio Espigüete to Vega de Cantos

Retrace the path back to Cardaño de Arriba and cross the river. Turn off to the left, passing by a few small houses, and continue in a northerly direction past some pretty waterfalls (approx. 1500m/4920ft), before reaching the Chozo de la Campiza hut, which is used by shepherds during the hot summer months. From the hut there is no recognizable path. Climb the ridge to the north of the hut for about 2km (1¼ miles), and then take a line in the direction of the small peak that sits above the right-hand side of the long rock band known as Agujas de Cardaño. Without going to the summit, traverse the peak in a northerly direction until reaching the saddle that separates it from the nearby Mojón de Tres Provincias. From the saddle,

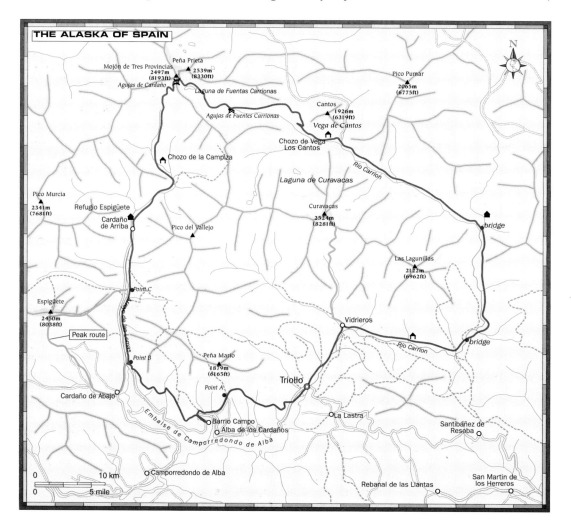

PEAK: ESPIGÜETE

From the summit of Espigüete there are unparalleled views of the Cordillera.

The starting point for attacking this peak is the village of Cardaño de Abajo.

From the highest point in the village take the jeep track, which gradually gains height as it traverses the southern flanks of Espigüete. After 4km (2½ miles), at a height of 1670m (5479ft), leave the track and climb the hillside, which becomes steeper and rockier with each step. You will eventually join the summit ridge, which leads to the summit a couple of hundred metres to the west.

From the top, the view can only be described as awesome. On a clear autumn's day, the views extend over nearly the whole of the Cordillera, including the Curavacas peak to the east. On the horizon all three massifs of the Picos de Europa form the backdrop to Peña Prieta in the north.

Looking south, the barren plains of Spain stretch as far as the Sierra Credos more than 200km (120 miles) in the distance.

The descent is down the rather delicate eastern arête, via the eastern summit of Espigüete, and finishes on the road to Cardaño de Arriba. Care should be taken, especially if it's wet or windy, as a certain amount of scrambling is involved on a few of the sections.

CLIMB ESSENTIALS

SUMMIT: Espigüete 2450m (8038ft).
CAMP: Cardaño de Abajo village.
GRADE: Scramble Grade 1.

---

a steep, somewhat loose descent over scree gives access to the Laguna de Fuentas Carrionas some 200m (650ft) below, in the valley of the same name. This marvellous, wild and romantic valley can be followed with some difficulty downstream until you reach a small hut. Just beyond the hut there is a jeep track, which you must follow for about 2km (1¼ miles) until it joins the main track through the Valle de Fuentas Carrionas. Turn right at the track and descend down to the wide Vega de Cantos where, next to the shepherds' huts, a camp can be set up for the night.

Looking to the west numerous waterfalls stream over the so-called *escaleras* (stairs) down the steep northern side of the Curavacas peak, which lies a short distance to the south and dominates the whole area. Here can also be seen many patches of uncovered turf, the aftermath of the night-time activities of the wild boar that hide during the day. Behind one of the large boulders at the base of the nearby rock face is a hidden spring.

Vega de Cantos to Triollo
Today is an easy stroll along the jeep track through

There are plenty of spots suitable for overnight camps in the Spanish Alaska.

the scenic Valle de Fuentas Carrionas, which is popular with walkers and mountain bikers alike. After crossing many rivulets and passing through the tiny hamlet of Vidrieros, the route leads back to the starting point of the trek in Triollo.

The route itself needs little explanation other than, at the point where the track fords the Río Carrion, a rocky path continues on the left-hand side of the valley through a small wood. After crossing a bridge over the Río Arauz the rocky path soon rejoins a jeep track.

A worthwhile extension to the day would be to visit the Pozo de Curavacas, which is only an hour's walk from the overnight camp at Vega de Cantos.

PEAK: PEÑA PRIETA

CLIMB ESSENTIALS

SUMMIT: Peña Prieta 2539m (8330ft).
CAMP: Cardaño de Arriba village.
GRADE: Scramble Grade 1.

Peña Prieta is the highest peak in the whole of the Cordillera.

From the saddle just before Mojón de Tres Provincias walk in a northerly direction up to the Mojón de Tres Provincias, a mere 200m (180yd) away. From here, take the obvious path east across another small saddle and then easily up to the summit of Peña Prieta a short distance away. Unlike its neighbouring peak, Espigüete, Peña Prieta has views of the Bay of Biscay in the distance.

Descend by reversing the same route back to the saddle.

Peña Prieta is subject to extreme climatic conditions, and snow can still be found on its summit as late in the year as May and June.

PEAK: CURAVACAS

From Triollo, the south face of Curavacas seems inconquerable; however, on closer inspection, the ascent is quite straightforward.

CLIMB ESSENTIALS

SUMMIT: Curavacas 2524m (8281ft).
CAMP: Vidrieros village.
GRADE: Scramble Grade 1.

An ascent of Curavacas is perhaps the most impressive of all three peaks that form the roof of the Cordillera.

In the middle of the small village of Vidrieros (1320m/4331ft), which is almost deserted throughout the winter months, take the Calle Chica from the village square; this soon becomes a jeep track. Follow this north-west until you cross a bridge over the Arroyo de Cabriles. From here a path goes off to the right up the stream, which is surrounded with bushes and isolated oaks. After approximately 1 hour a small alpine pasture, El Resollar (1550m/5085ft), is reached at the foot of the majestic Curavacas.

Follow a path surrounded by boulders over some scree. Before reaching the col that lies ahead, enter the steep gully known as the Callego Grande (2100m/6890ft) off to the left. Be careful not to climb all the way up to the pass as no route leads up to the summit from there. The route up through the gully, between gigantic boulders, is marked with cairns and gains height quickly. Towards the top of the gully is an obvious grassy col, pass to the left-hand side of this and continue up the gully. In a few places it's necessary to scramble.

Near the top there is another col which this time you do approach. From the col, a path goes round the north side of the summit and then up to the top, where there is a cross and a trig. point.

Descend via the same route, but be aware that in cloudy conditions the route down is difficult.

TREK 12: THE SAJA AND BESAYA NATIONAL RESERVE

The Saja and Besaya National Reserve extends east of the Picos de Europa along the northern slopes of the Cordillera Cantábrica, between the coast and the Ebro reservoir. To the west it is bordered by the 2600-m (8530-ft) Picos de Europa, to the south by the 2200-m (7220-ft) Sierra del Cordell and to the north-west by the Peña Sagra. The reserve contains one of the largest beech and oak forests in Cantabria and, at 181 square kilometres, is the largest national reserve in Spain. Here, in the heart of Green Spain, the rainfall is high, filling the numerous rivers and streams – such as the Deva, the Nansa, the Saja and the Besaya – which run through the woods and valleys to drain into the Bay of Biscay.

TREK ESSENTIALS

LENGTH: 4 days; 73km (43¾ miles).
ACCESS: From Santander or Bilbao take the motorway west towards Oviedo as far as Cabezon de la Sal. Here, take the CA180 towards Reinosa, and 2km (1¼ miles) after the tiny village of Fresneda turn left onto the CA280 to Barcena Mayor. From Palencia or Burgos head for Reinosa, and then take the C625 to Alto Campoo. A few kilometres from Alto Campoo take a right at a crossroads (towards Cabezon de la Sal and Saja). Cross the Palombero pass and turn right at a crossroads before Saja for Barcena Mayor.
DIFFICULTY: Moderate.
HIGHEST POINT: El Hilton col 1553m (5095ft).
TREK STYLE: Bivouac and hotels/*albergues*.
MAPS: Mapa del Comarca 1:50 000 Saja/Nansa (Cantabria).
FURTHER OPTIONS: Alternative route available from Collado de Sejos to the village of Puente Pumar.

The romantic Pozo del Amo flows through the heart of the Saja and Besaya National Reserve.

Until recently the only sources of income for the local people in the remote valleys were farming and a few insignificant mines. Life was hard and due to depopulation many villages were on the verge of extinction. Today, however, tourism has

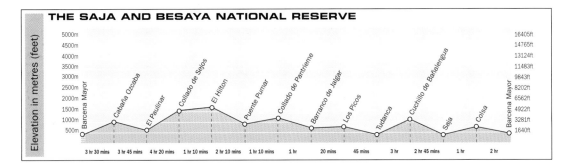

THE SAJA AND BESAYA NATIONAL RESERVE

Elevation in metres (feet)

Barcena Mayor	Cabaña Orzaba	El Paulinar	Collado de Sejos	El Hilton	Puente Pumar	Collado de Pantriene	Barranco de Jalgar	Los Picos	Tudanca	Cuchillo de Bañalengua	Saja	Colsa	Barcena Mayor	

| 3 hr 30 mins | 3 hr 45 mins | 4 hr 20 mins | 1 hr 10 mins | 2 hr 10 mins | 1 hr 10 mins | 1 hr | 20 mins | 45 mins | 3 hr | 2 hr 45 mins | 1 hr | 2 hr |

provided a new lease of life to picturesque villages such as Barcena Mayor and Carmona in the nearby Nansa valley. Many of their marvellous farmhouses, built in the original Cantabrian style, have been converted into *casas rurales*. These houses have great character – they are big buildings with, generally, a stable on the ground floor and stone arches forming the entrance; the living accommodation is on the first and second floors and they normally

Author Ilja Schröder with his trusty companion Nalin next to the Tramburrios rapids of the Río Saja.

have south-facing balconies and red-tiled roofs; attached to the side of the building would normally be a wood-burning oven for making bread. Today, Turismo Rural (Ecotourism) has taken over the region and, at least during the summer months, the villages are once again populated.

Barcena Mayor to Palombera

From the pretty village of Barcena Mayor, where it's possible to stock up on all sorts of local goodies, such as red deer or wild boar chorizo, take the village road south-west and cross the Barranco Queriendo. Follow the road and the river for about

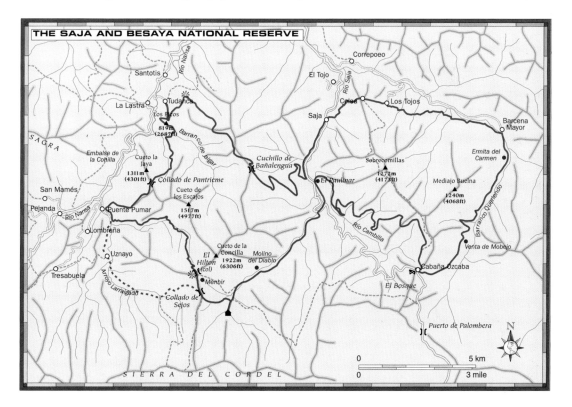

FLORA AND FAUNA OF THE SAJA AND BESAYA NATIONAL RESERVE

The seemingly endless, forested northern slopes of the Cordillera Cantábrica were almost forgotten by civilization, so many unusual species of flora and fauna have survived to this day. The woods consist mainly of beech (*Fagus sylvatica*) and oak (*Quercus*) intermixed with chestnut (*Castanea sativa*) and cherry (*Prunus*). The sub-growth is made up mainly of holly (*Ilex aquifolium*) and hazel bushes (*Carylus avellana*), but also many herbs, such as bell heath (*Daboecia cantabrica*), exist along with ferns.

The most important mammals are without doubt the wolf (*Canis lupus*) and Brown bear (*Ursus arctos*); these species cause many heated and intense discussions between farmers, hunters and wildlife conservationists alike. Furthermore, there are a considerable number of red deer (*Cervus elaphus*) which were introduced after the Civil War (1936–39), and chamoix (*Rupicapra rupicapra*) are found on the more mountainous terrain. One can also see numerous Roe deer (*Capreolus capreolous*), wild boar (*Sus scrofa*), foxes and badgers (*Meles meles*).

It is far more difficult to see the shy wildcats (*Felis silvestris*) or even an otter (*Lutra lutra*) in one of the numerous brooks and rivulets. In the bird

The now-protected holly bush (*Ilex aquifolium*), whose berries come out in the early winter months, can be found in the woodlands of the northern Cordillera.

world the endangered turkey-like capercaillie (*Tetrao urogallus*) is surely the most unusual, along with the rare Black woodpecker (*Dryocopus martius*) and Golden (*Aquila chrysaetos*) and Booted (*Hieraaetus pennatus*) eagles and Griffon (*Gyps fulvus*) and Egyptian vultures (*Neophron percnopterus*).

Although evidence of wild boar (*Sus scrofa*) is often found on treks, actually spotting these shy creatures is far more difficult.

The Saja and Besaya National Reserve is famous for its Red deer (*Cervus elaphus*), particularly their enormous antlers.

The Saja and Besaya National Reserve is full of heavily wooded mountains. Beyond the reserve, the jagged cliffs of the Picos de Europa are just visible in the distance.

1km (⅔ mile) through woodland up to the Ermita del Carmen chapel, where the road ends. From here, follow the valley on a well-trodden path above the river, crossing a few side valleys and passing by some old barns, Venta de Mobejo. Continue on a jeep track up to the road pass of Peurto de Palombera (1000m/3280ft). Cross the road and climb the slope south-eastwards for a few metres to reach a small hut; this will provide basic shelter for the night.

Palombera to Shepherd's Hut
In fine weather the sunrises from this small hut are worth setting your alarm for. Return back down to the road and follow the previous day's trek for 300m (270yd) before turning left and after a further kilometre turn left again. In the early hours, as the first rays of light hit the meadows, Red deer and wild boar can be seen returning from a night of foraging in the undergrowth.

The track is now easily followed through pleasant beech forest. After a further 2km (1⅓ miles), just beyond a small hut on a shoulder, is a junction. Take the track that descends to the left to the Río Cambilla. A few more kilometres further down the valley, the track passes by an old

disused water-mill (El Paulinar), beside which you take a sharp left southwards. Climb straight up the hillside until you reach a road pass. Cross over the pass and take the obvious path that lies ahead.

Follow the course of the roaring Río Saja up the Valle de Infierno. Forest eventually gives way to open countryside and the path crosses a small wooden bridge, Puente de la Robleda. Shortly after, a small valley enters from the north-west and the path disappears. Due to the absence of a path, in poor conditions it is necessary to use a compass – go due south up a hill. After approximately 0.5km (⅓ mile) you will join a jeep track. Turn left downhill and follow the track until it crosses a river. Cross the river, and just beyond it take a little path south for about 100m (110yd) to the refuge. During the evening, deer can be seen rutting.

Shepherd's Hut to Tudanca
Return back down to the track, turn left and follow it for about 15 minutes until it turns towards the south. From here you must hike cross-country on a boulder-strewn slope for nearly 1km (⅔ mile) westwards to a jeep track. Once on the track turn right and follow it gently down to Collado de Sejos

Near the source of the Río Saja, the Puente de la Robleda must be crossed on the second day of the trek.

(1504m/4934ft). From here, there are breathtaking views over the northern Cordillera and on a clear day the majestic Picos de Europa stand out on the horizon in the west.

From the col, there are two alternatives. The first is to go north-west on the signposted jeep track down through the Larraigado valley, passing through the village of Uznayo, to Puente Pumar at the southern end of the Embalse de la Cohilla reservoir. The other option is to take the path that leads off to the north. On this route you will pass collapsed Bronze Age menhir megaliths (standing stones), evidence of the earliest inhabitants of this wild region. On reaching another col, El Hilton, take a jeep track down into Puente Pumar.

From Puente Pumar, take the track that passes the church and makes its way up to the radio tower on top of Cueto la Jaya peak (1311m/4301ft). Just before the top, near the Collado de Pantrieme on a sharp left-hand bend in the track, a path goes off downhill in a north-easterly direction.

After crossing a little valley the path joins another jeep track. Follow the track down past numerous little barns scattered across the hillside. After passing the Barranco de Jalgar continue up and over the small ridge of Los Picos. From the other side of the ridge the track goes down to Tudanca, a village not only well known for its 19th-century *palacio* (nobleman's house) but also for its local breed of cow. Tudanca cows have been used over the centuries as working animals and are noted for their extremely large horns. At Tudanca you can stay either in the hotel, the *albergue* or in a *casa rurale*.

Tudanca to Barcena Mayor

Leave the village and return back up the previous day's track. After about 1km (⅔ mile), take a left turn and follow a track over the Alto de la Jazona, down through the Cuchillo de Bañalengua and into a pretty beech forest that joins the main C625 road. Walk along the road northwards down to the village of Saja. A path behind the village church leads up the hillside to another little village, Colsa. Follow the road for about 1km (⅔ mile) and, just before entering Los Tojos, take the track that heads off to the east; this will lead you back to Barcena Mayor.

In the Collado de Sejos remains of Bronze Age menhirs can be found.

CORDILLERA CANTÁBRICA DIRECTORY

GETTING THERE

By air: Bilbao is the most convenient airport for the Cordillera Cantábrica. This airport is served by many different airlines including British Airways, Go and Iberia. The high season for tickets is July and August, Easter and Christmas. If you're booking quite far in advance, look out for cheap deals on Go.
British Airways: www.britishairways.com
Go Airlines: www.go-fly.com
Iberia Airlines: www.iberia.com

By train: Train services run to and from Oviedo and Santander, the main access points for the Cordillera Cantábrica. To confirm train times, contact:
Bilbao Train Station: C/Gurtubay 1; tel. 944 395077
Bilbao Termíbus station: tel. 944 395205
Oviedo Train Station: C/Urías; tel. 985 250202
Santander Train Station: Plaza Estaciones; tel. 942 210211
RENFE, Barcelona: tel. 93 4900202

By bus: There are regular services to Oviedo and Santander from Madrid. To confirm bus times, contact:
Bilbao Bus Station: C/Hurtado de Amezaga; tel. 944 238623
Bilbao Termíbus station: tel. 944 395205
Oviedo Bus Station: Plaza Primo de Rivera 1; tel. 85 281200
Santander Bus Station: Plaza Estaciones; tel. 942 211995

ACCOMMODATION
Manned Refuge
Albergue de Barcena Mayor: tel. 908 186657

TOURIST INFORMATION
Cantábrica Tourist information: Plaza de Velarde 1, Santander; tel. 942 818000

Burgos: Plaza de Alonso Martínez 7; tel. 947 203125
Oviedo: Plaza de Alfonso II El casto; tel. 985 213385
Puente Nansa: tel. 942 728001
Reinosa: Avda de la Puente
San Vicente de La Barquera: Avda Generalísimo 20; tel. 942 710797
Santander: Plaza Porticada; tel. 942 310708
Tudanca: tel. 942 729002
Valle de Carbueniga: tel. 942 706001

EMERGENCY NUMBERS
Emergency Services: tel. 112
Guardia Civil: tel. 062

The Peña Prieta massif is just one section of the vast mountains that make up the Cordillera Cantábrica.

7
PICOS DE EUROPA

Trekkers and climbers have long frequented the Picos de Europa, drawn to the region by its challenging peaks, such as the monolithic Naranjo de Bulnes, spectacular long-distance trails and famous Cares Gorge (Garganta del Cares).

Three massifs – Western, Central and Eastern – make up this mountain range, which itself is part of the Cordillera Cantábrica. Each massif has its own characteristics, from the lunar landscapes of the Central to the slightly more gentle surroundings of the Eastern and the high summer pastures of the Western, all of which are tackled in the treks covered in this chapter.

The unmistakable monlith of El Naranjo de Bulnes, otherwise known as Pico Urriello, rises up to dominate the Picos de Europa.

An interesting way to travel to Spain is on one of the two ferry services that cross the Bay of Biscay to arrive on the Iberian peninsula's northern shores. Approaching Spain on a clear winter's day, a large part of the Cordillera Cantábrica is visible on the horizon from a great distance, but one section stands out like no other among its neighbours – the jagged, snow-capped towers that form the Picos de Europa.

The Picos lie only 20km (12 miles) inland from the coast and acquired their name, the 'Peaks of Europe', by being the first European landmass to be sighted and serving as a reference point to early seafarers returning from long fishing trips or perhaps even from the Americas. In 1918, the western massif of this range became Spain's first national park, which on 30 May 1995 was enlarged to include all three massifs – the Picos de Europa is now the largest national park in the country.

Geological Origins

The origin of the Picos is largely identical to that of other European mountain ranges, such as the Alps or the Pyrenees. During the various ice ages, the moving glaciers modelled the largest mass of limestone in Europe and this, along with the process of underground drainage, has given them their unique karst appearance. The melting glaciers and precipitation have etched out a labyrinth of deep shafts and immeasurable cave systems below the surface, many of which are still unexplored.

The Three Massifs

Today, the Picos de Europa is divided into three distinct massifs, the Western massif, or El Cornion, between the ravines of the Sella and Cares rivers; the Central massif, or Los Urrielles, between the ravines of the Cares and Duje rivers; and the Eastern massif, or Andara, between the

This famous wolf trap, 'El Chorco del Lobo', near the village of Caín caught its last victim in 1975.

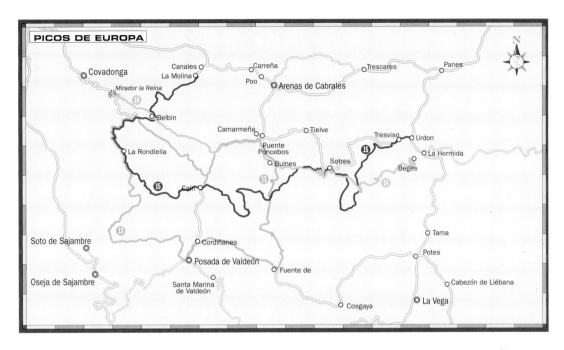

ravines of the Deva and Duje rivers. The Central massif, which is the highest of the three, has become a Mecca for climbers from round the world, with its distinctive peaks such as Pico Urriello (2519m/8265ft) – also known as El Naranjo de Bulnes – Peña Vieja (2613m/8573ft), and Torre de Cerredo, which at 2648m (8688ft) is the highest mountain in the Picos de Europa.

Local Flora and Fauna

These rugged limestone peaks interspersed with deep lush valleys provide cover for a vast checklist of animal and plant life. Vultures and eagles are not uncommon and animals such as the chamois, the rarely seen wild boar, and even the wolf and the European Brown bear still live here, while the lower foothills are a richly stocked habitat for a great variety of flora.

Equally impressive are the deep gorges of the Sella, Cares and Deva rivers. Their rock walls rise vertically for over 2000m (6500ft) in places. These unusual geographical features meant that, until recently, the valleys, villages and their inhabitants were largely cut off from the rest of the world. The isolating effects of the long, hard winters forced the people of the Picos de Europa to become mainly self sufficient, resulting in a culture that has changed little over the centuries.

One of the last remaining watermills used for the cleaning and flattening of wool fibres is to be found in Liebana.

TREK 13: LUNAR LANDSCAPES OF THE PICOS DE EUROPA

'The mountain was in its beginning; slender pinnacles, tapering needles and graceful towers had still not risen from its surface. These refinements of its architecture were hidden in its depths, like a work of art trapped in the heart of a block of marble: And the supreme Artist would have to work for thousands of years before revealing the great marvel of his enormous sculpture.'

This description of the Picos de Europa was taken from the journals of Pedro Pidal, the first person to summit El Naranjo de Bulnes in 1904 and the principal instigator for the formation of the Picos de Europa National Park in 1918.

TREK ESSENTIALS

LENGTH: 8 days.
ACCESS: From Santander, take the motorway in the direction of Oviedo and leave at Unquera. Take the N621 through Potes and on to Fuente De.
DIFFICULTY: Strenuous.
HIGHEST POINT: Torre de Horcados Rojos (2506/8222ft).
TREK STYLE: Refuges and hotels.
MAPS: Adrados Ediciones 1:25 000 Picos de Europa Macizo Occidental, Picos de Europa Macizo Central.
FURTHER OPTIONS: Ascent of Pico Tesorero (2570m/8432ft).

Fuente De to Refugio Ubeda

The starting point is the cable-car station at Fuente De, next to the Parador Nacional de Deva, about 23km (13¾ miles) west of Potes. Take the cable car and in just 3 minutes you will have ascended 800m (2625ft) to the upper station. From El Cable there are spectacular views of the Liebana valley far below.

A good track heads off in a north-easterly directions and after about 10 minutes there is a junction to the left. Take this track and follow it along the base of the buttresses that form the bottom of the enormous Peña Vieja massif up to the Cabaña Verónica. This curious little building was once a gun turret on a battleship and was reputedly carried up by climbers in sections, as a joke; it has now been concreted into position and provides accommodation for up to six people and is manned all year!

From the hut, the trek continues north for a short distance until ending abruptly on the edge of a large drop, the Torre de Horcados Rojos (2506m/8222ft). It is quite common to see many Alpine choughs playing in the thermals and updrafts and, with a bit of luck, you may even spot the distinctive wallcreeper, with its butterfly-like flight, in among the surrounding rock faces.

The way down lies over to the right, where a steel cable assists a steep descent into the Jou de los Boches. Take particular care here as stones knocked down from above have been the cause of several accidents. From the bottom of this glacial basin a 360-degree panorama of towering peaks awaits.

At first the path goes through the middle of the depression and is easily followed, due to the many

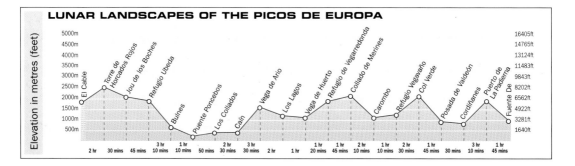

LUNAR LANDSCAPES OF THE PICOS DE EUROPA

cairns marking the way. The route then moves over to the right, up a loose section and eventually climbs out on the other side up a short, easy gully. From this point there is a classic view of Pico Urriello, more commonly known as El Naranjo de Bulnes, with its towering 550-m (1804-ft) west face clearly visible.

It takes about 20 minutes to walk down the obvious path to the Refugio Ubeda (1960m/6430ft) located just below El Naranjo. This well-equipped refuge is manned all year and it can get extremely busy in the summer months when it's worth booking in advance. In the evening, the usually timid chamoix, now accustomed to the presence of humans, approach the hut looking for food.

Refugio Ubeda to Bulnes

Leaving the hut, a vague path heads off due north (don't take the better-marked path that heads north-east towards Sotres) and quickly descends to a point where it appears to end at a small cliff. At the bottom of the cliff, a steep gully goes down to the right. Just to the left of this gully, descend a short climb, which in the bottom can have snow until late June.

The way on is not obvious at first. Looking across the gully, some cairns mark the way up a short easy climb, follow these cairns. From the top of the climb, the path then drops into a small gully and, after making its way through an area of large boulders, descends diagonally over scree for some time until turning west to reach the top of the Camburero gully. Follow this gully down over further loose scree and after about 150m (165yd), you should be able to hear water below the surface. A little cave gives access to the water should you need it. Continue down the gully and exit near the bottom on the right-hand side.

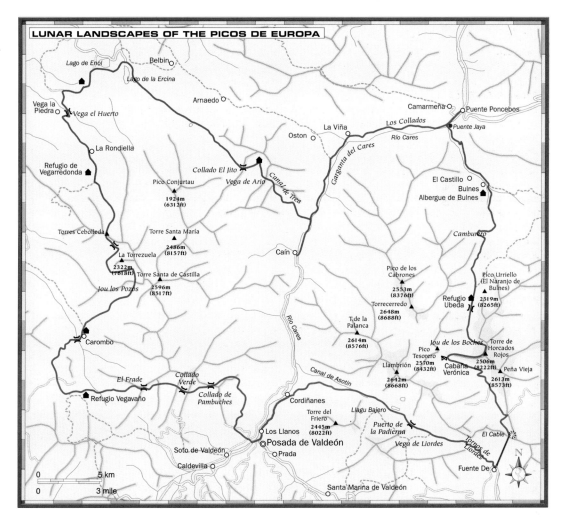

LUNAR LANDSCAPES OF THE PICOS DE EUROPA

One of the most popular destinations in the Picos de Europa are the lakes of Covadonga, including Lago de la Ercina. The summits of the Western massif form a magical backdrop to the lake.

The trek now heads into the Balcosin valley, which has a good path through it. At one point, the valley narrows and ends in a small waterfall. Cross over the top of the waterfall and climb down on the right-hand side. Continue down the valley until, once again, it narrows and another waterfall appears. A steep muddy ramp leads down to the bottom of the waterfall; however, the easier option is to take the less obvious route over to the right. This route doubles back on itself behind an outcrop and then joins the bottom of the ramp. Cross a little stream and after a few minutes the village of Bulnes will come into view just below. Accommodation can be found in either the Refugio Peña Main or in the newly refurbished and recommended Albergue de Bulnes.

The idyllic mountain village of Bulnes was, until recently, isolated from the rest of the world, reachable only on a narrow, vertiginous donkey track. Today, an underground funicular railway connects it through a 2.4-km (1½-mile) tunnel to Puente Poncebos, way below in the Cares Gorge (Garganta del Cares). Accommodation can also be found in Puente Poncebos.

Bulnes to Caín

Note: It is possible to trek all the way from Bulnes to Vega de Ario in one long day if time is restricted.

Cross the little bridge and turn left past the remains of the church to follow an old but good path all the way down to the Cares Gorge, which is reached via the pretty Roman bridge of Puente del Jaya. On reaching the road, turn left and after about 200m (220yd) take a path that doubles back on itself and up to the right. (Do not stay on the lower path as this ends after 2km/1¼ miles.) This well-maintained path, which was constructed as part of a hydro scheme, ascends for about 45 minutes and then levels off for the remainder of its 12-km (7¼-mile) course.

Nearing the end of the path, you must cross the crystal-clear and icy waters of the Río Cares, some 120m (390ft) below, on newly constructed bridges, and then pass through a section of tunnels before emerging into the picturesque village of Caín with its many small hotels and bed-and-breakfasts (pensions).

Caín to Vega de Ario

It's necessary to backtrack along the Cares Gorge until you are 15m (15yd) beyond the fourth bridge; here, a fairly unobvious rocky path ascends steeply through a beech forest on a series of zigzags until breaking out into the open Canal de Trea gully. In the gully take the steep path that leads to a small spring emerging from beneath a large boulder. The path continues up on the right of the spring, avoiding a scree slope on the left, and goes up a narrow gully to join a small ridge, which is ascended to eventually reach the Collado de Las Cruzes.

From the col the way on to the refuge at Vega de Ario is north and is marked with cairns and the occasional dash of paint. The views across the 1000-m (3280-ft) deep Cares Gorge and the Central massif beyond as the sun goes down are breathtaking.

Vega de Ario to Refugio de Vegarredonda

Leave the refuge on the well-marked path that heads south-west. You will quickly reach the Collado El Jito, with its brass plaque showing the locations of various surrounding peaks and landmarks. The route now turns to the north-west and is easily followed all the way down to the lakes of Covadonga – Lago de la Ercina and Lago de Enol.

Crystal clear and wild, the waters of the Río Cares force their way through the Picos de Europa.

From Lago de la Ercina climb the little ridge behind the bar at the car-park to get a fantastic view of Lago de Enol. Follow the path round the southern shores of Enol until you join a jeep track. Turn left on the track and follow it for about 20 minutes to an obvious junction. Turn left, and trek through beech forest until the track ends and a well-trodden path, which leads directly to the Refugio de Vegarredonda, begins. The refuge is reached in about 1½ hours. After dinner, take time to enjoy the unique mountain sunset and the peaceful surroundings.

Refugio de Vegarredonda to Refugio Vegavaño

Head south from the refuge to an old ruined hut. From here, take the path that leads up the Vegarredonda gully. After passing a section of zigzags the path splits; take the right-hand option. Continue through a small col and then head south up broken terrain on a wide slope to the Collado de Merines. Follow the path that runs below the summit of Torres Cebolleda until you reach a small spring below its south-west face. Now go south, without losing height, round the north-west spur of La Torrezuela peak and continue round, over a little shoulder and down a short ridge, until reaching a large depression on the south side of the peak.

Ascend the marked path on the left-hand side of the depression to the Jou los Pozos.

From Jou los Pozos take the path that goes down to the left, traversing the scree slope diagonally. Just before the Corpus Christie Pinnacle, leave the path and head south-west across an area of large blocks and sharp protrusions. Trend slightly up to a small shoulder but always staying high on the right. The route descends over scree until it becomes grassy and steeper. When it becomes impossible to continue down, turn right and about 50m (55yd) away, an easy gully descends to the Carombo pastures. From behind some barns, take the path that leads into the forest and, after crossing the Río Dobra, ascend steeply to a jeep track above. Follow the track for a short distance to a clearing from where you will see the Refugio Vegavaño.

Refugio Vegavaño to Posada de Valdeón

Climb through an old beech-wood in an easterly direction up to the El Frade col. There are marvellous views to the north-east back into the Upper Dobra valley, while in front extensive woodland spreads across the Valdeón valley. Cross the col and head due east across a short scree slope to gain a wide grassy terrace known as the Travesona. After passing the Collado Verde, the path becomes vague; stay high up on the left following the cairns for a short distance until the path becomes more visible. After passing the Collado de Pambuches, descend the gully of the same name in zigzags to soon arrive at a spring. The route now passes some barns on its descent to Posada de Valdeón, where there are numerous hotels and pensions.

Posada de Valdeón to Fuente Dé

Follow the road from Posada de Valdeón down to the village of Cordiñanes. At the left-hand bend in the middle of the village a path goes off to the right and after some 200m (220yd) splits. Take the right-hand track, which ascends on scree before entering a vertiginous balcony and continuing up between rocky outcrops. Beyond is a beech forest, where the route becomes less steep. Continue to ascend in a south-easterly direction up the Canal de Asotin, eventually passing Llagu Bajero and reaching Puerto de la Padierna (1971m/6467ft).

Cross the col and continue heading south-east, rocky outcrops will appear on your left, to reach the Vega de Liordes, with its deserted mines. This is a particularly good place during the autumn and winter months to spot agile chamoix performing unbelievable climbing feats. Continue in an easterly direction and soon a steep zigzagging path – known as the Tornos de Liordes and once used by donkeys to bring zinc ore from the mines to the valley bottom – leads all the way back to the starting point at Fuente De, deep below in the valley.

PEAK: TESORERO

Tesorero peak lies north-west of Cabaña Verónica. It is easily climbed in just over 1 hour from the hut and offers not only an exceptional viewpoint for the Central massif, but its summit is also the convergence of the three provinces of Cantabria, Asturias and León.

From the hut, follow the route, which is well-marked with cairns, that goes north-west easily to the top. Care should be taken on the upper section as there is a certain amount of loose rock.

Descent is by the same route.

CLIMB ESSENTIALS

SUMMIT: Tesorero 2570m (8432ft).
CAMP: Cabaña Verónica.
GRADE: Scramble Grade 1.

From the easily attained summit of Tesorero you will be able to take in views of almost the entire Central massif.

TREK 14: THE FLIGHT OF THE ARABS

'Here, in the name of the Mother of God, from amongst the rocks, on top of the summits, Spain emerged.'

Cayetano Enríquez de Salamanca

The above quote refers to the famous defeat of the Moors at Covadonga in AD722. With their leader dead, the crushed remains of the Arab army disbanded and were forced to retreat in a disorganized manner while the Christian forces, under the command of Don Pelayo, gave chase. One of the routes they took apparently crossed all three massifs of the Picos de Europa, passing through beautiful *majadas* (summer pastures for grazing cattle, with the occasional small hut), crossing the deep Cares Gorge and passing nearby the now famous El Naranjo de Bulnes (Pico Urriello). On this relatively easy trek it is not possible to follow the exact route taken by the Moors, but you will still cover all three massifs of the Picos de Europa.

TREK ESSENTIALS

LENGTH: 4 days; 50km (31¼ miles).
ACCESS: From Oviedo take the N634 towards Santander but leave to reach Cangas de Onis. Head west from Cangas de Onis and then turn right to Covadonga.
DIFFICULTY: Strenuous to tough.
HIGHEST POINT: Casetón de Andara 1720m (5643ft).
TREK STYLE: Bivouac.
MAPS: Ediciones Adrados 1:25,000 Picos de Europa Macizo Occidental, Picos de Europa Macizo Central.
FURTHER OPTIONS: On the fourth day of the trek it is possible to climb many of the easier peaks in the Eastern massif, the easiest being Pico del Mancondiú (2000m/6562ft).

Mirador de la Reina to Puente Poncebos

The Mirador de la Reina (Queen's Viewpoint) is located about 6km (3⅔ miles) from the Sanctuary of Covadonga on the road to Los Lagos (The Lakes). Just to the left of the mirador, looking north, take a small path that leads to a jeep track below. The track goes directly below the mirador and passes a vulture-feeding point, where, at the right time of day, numerous Griffon vultures feed on the dead remains of cattle left there by a local conservation group (FAPAS).

The track continues over Collado Uberdón – northwards there are views of the Sierra de

The stark barren summits of the Central massif often resemble a lunar landscape.

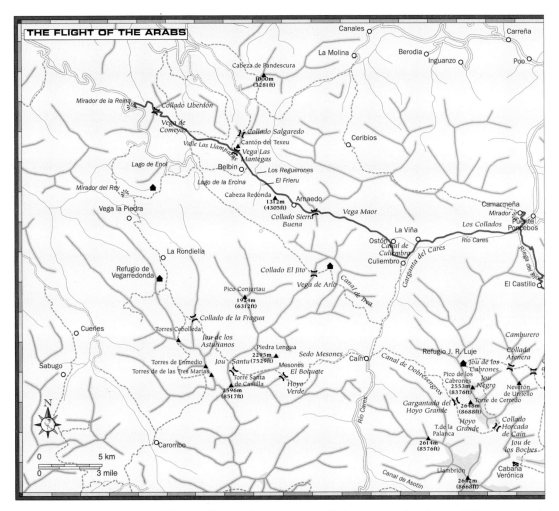

THE FLIGHT OF THE ARABS

Cubeta, which separates the Picos de Europa from the coast – and then drops down into the wide open and lush Vega de Comeyas depression. The track comes to an abrupt halt in the middle of the depression at the remains of old mine workings.

To the east, at the far end of the Valle Las Llampazas, is the square-topped peak of Cantón del Texeu; this is the way to head. The route is vague all the way to the base of the peak but, unless it is misty, route finding should be simple.

At the base of the peak, take the good cobbled path to the right, which, after passing through the Cantón col, drops down into Vega Las Mantegas. The path now disappears, but continue across grassy pastures. After a few hundred metres, a rocky path going over a small shoulder gives

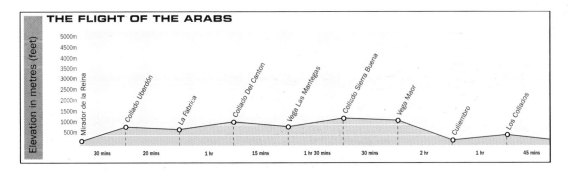

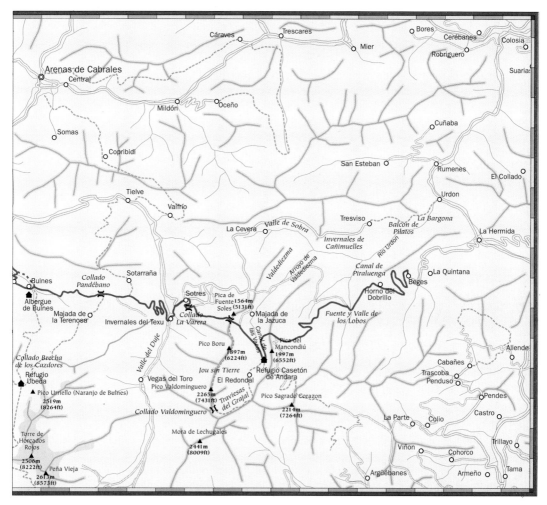

access to the nearby summer settlement of Belbin. It is worth detouring to Belbin, as it has a good spring, and you may have the opportunity to buy some superb local cheese direct from the farmers.

The trek, however, continues through the *vega* (meadow) and the path soon reappears. Eventually you will drop down the side of a small hill and follow the course of the somewhat dried up Los Reguerones stream. At the point where the valley becomes more open and flat the path crosses the stream and starts to climb gently. After passing by the well-hidden El Frieru spring the path splits – head to the right, traversing diagonally up the hillside. Trek north of Cabeza Redonda peak and continue up, past a group of shepherds' huts, to

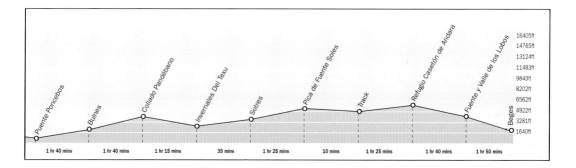

Evidence of the first conquest of Spain can be found in the form of numerous Roman bridges that were once part of a network of paths known as Las Calzadas Romanas.

the wide Collado Sierra Buena. From the other side of the col, descend into the valley and after about 1km (⅔ mile), in the middle of a large depression, the huts of Vega Maor come into view. From the huts head east and climb out of the depression.

Soon the path splits, but either option can be taken, as they both lead, after about 1½ km (1 mile), down to the inhabited summer pastures of Ostón. From this beautiful *majada*, perched high above the Cares Gorge, the views down to the river below with a backdrop of the Central massif are stunning.

From Ostón's southernmost group of barns descend through zigzags down a gully before turning left into the Culiembro gully. You will eventually join the Ruta del Cares (Cares Gorge path) way below. Turn left onto the Ruta del Cares and follow it easily for about 6km (3⅔ mile). After passing Los Collados, descend gently to the road below and turn left towards the hamlet of

Puente Poncebos. Poncebos, which is reached after passing through a small tunnel, is graced with two hostels and a hotel. The nearby village of Arenas de Cabrales (10 minutes by taxi) also has numerous hotels.

Puente Poncebos to Sotres
Walk back up the road towards the Cares Gorge and, just after the tunnel, a well-marked path descends on the left down to the Roman bridge, Puente del Jaya. Cross the Río Cares and soon cross a more modern bridge, Puente del Jardu. A somewhat vertiginous path starts to climb the steep-sided gorge of Riega del Tejo. This is easily followed as it was once the main access to the remote mountain village of Bulnes.

After about an hour the valley levels off and you can cross the river on a small bridge and follow the path up to El Castillo (Upper Bulnes). However, if time is at a premium, continue along the river, with-

The whole of the Picos de Europa offers marvellous opportunities for walking, and there are endless breathtaking views, such as this one of El Naranjo de Bulnes.

out crossing the bridge, and after passing the entrance to the funicular railway on the left cross a small bridge into the busy (summer only) little hamlet of Bulnes.

After stopping for refreshments in one of the three bars, leave the village re-crossing the bridge next to the village square and take the path to the right, which passes just below a small cave entrance.

The route now takes an obvious path, passing by several *majadas* dotted with their typical shepherds' huts. After about ½ hour you will spot the stunning El Naranjo de Bulnes, way up above the Varera forest. This impressive monolithic mountain should perhaps be described as infamous rather than famous – a first ascent of it was not made until 1904, and since then it has claimed the lives of numerous climbers over the decades. El Naranjo de Bulnes is probably the most difficult climbing peak on the Spanish penin-

sula and many of the routes on its towering 550-m (1804-ft) west face are considered some of the finest technical routes in the world.

After crossing the stream for the second time on stepping stones, the route passes below a rocky outcrop on the left. Just beyond the outcrop, in a wooded area where irises grow, take a turning to the left (if you miss this turning you will quickly arrive at a barn). Soon the path breaks out of the forest into an open valley. Follow the path up to the Collado Pandébano and then descend west. After passing two small huts you will join a jeep track just below. Turn left on to the jeep track and follow it all the way down to the Invernales del Texu in the Valle del Duje.

Beyond the buildings there is a junction in the track; take the left-hand option and you will soon join a road. Turn right on to the road, this will take you via steep hairpin bends up to Sotres. Sotres, at 1045m (3428ft) is the highest village in the province of Asturias. Accommodation can be found in one of the several hotels or bed and breakfasts.

Sotres to Beges

In the main street of Sotres is the bar/hotel Casa Cipriano. To the right of the bar is a concrete uphill track leaving the village heading south. Take this track, ignoring the first two turnings on the left, the second of which is next to a steep slab of rocks used by local climbers. The track continues up but soon levels off somewhat at the Collado Varera. After passing some barns, take the second turning on the right, just below a little peak (Pica de Fuente Soles), and follow the track steeply up until you reach a flat grassy area behind the aforementioned small peak. From here a steep slope rises in a south-easterly direction and a vague path follows the line of the small stream that runs down the hill. Follow the path/stream, and shortly you will pass a flat area where cotton-grass flourishes.

The path soon becomes more obvious, eventually leading to the ridge due south of Pica de Fuente Soles. Looking back, the views of the Central massif more than compensate for the effort of the ascent. From the ridge, a path descends due east down to a jeep track. Turn right at the track and gently ascend to Refugio Casetón de Andara. The refuge is located on a scree slope just after a rusty iron railway bridge you will have passed under. The railway was once used for removing ore from one of the many zinc mines to be found in this area. The refuge, which once belonged to one of the mining companies, now serves as a base for many ascents in the Eastern massif. East of the hut is the steep west face of Pica del Mancondiú, an ascent of which is easily accomplished via its south col, and then by climbing or scrambling the somewhat exposed path that goes up the southern side (1 hour from Casetón de Andara).

From the refuge the trek heads round the north side of the Pica del Mancondiú. On reaching the other side of the peak start to descend gently. After passing through a beech forest you will emerge into open countryside in Fuente y Valle de los Lobos (Valley of the Wolves), where a good spring is located next to the track. In this area it's easy to spot Alpine newts and fire salamanders hiding under rocks.

The next section of the trek is flat and runs parallel to the Canal de Urdon gorge. On reaching the top of the Canal de Piraluenga gully, the icy-cold waters of the Río Urdon can be seen some 850m (2789ft) below. Looking across to the other side of the gorge the unbelievable, gravity-defying, zigzagging path that leads from the hydro plant at Urdon to the remote village of Tresviso is clearly visible. The track now starts to descend again and, after passing some more (ruined) mine buildings, you will head through a series of hairpins before eventually reaching the little village of Beges. From Beges a taxi can be taken to Potes or Panes.

Old shepherds' huts such as this will be passed as you walk through the majadas, *summer pastures, on this trek.*

TREK 15: THE SUMMITS OF THE THREE MASSIFS

This trek has surely to be the most all-embracing adventure accomplishable in the Picos. It covers all three massifs and includes an optional ascent of the highest peaks in each one. Starting more or less from sea level and going up to the summit of the highest peak, it covers the complete range of terrain, scenery, flora and fauna to be found in the spectacular Picos de Europa National Park.

Urdon to Tresviso

Starting from the hydro plant by the side of the road at Urdon, a wide path heads off below the towering walls of the Urdon gorge. Beyond the small 'Hydro', cross the clear waters of the Río Urdon and follow the left bank of the river. A short distance on, a rusty monorail ascends the side of the gorge almost vertically; this railway was used many years ago during the construction of a high-level canal to feed water to the hydro. The path now crosses two more bridges, after which the character of the walk changes dramatically.

The summits of the Central and Eastern massifs stand proud above the clouds to tower over the wide and fertile Liebana valley.

TREK ESSENTIALS

LENGTH: 7 days; 77.75km (46½ miles).
ACCESS: From Santander, take the motorway in the direction of Oviedo and leave at Unquera. Take the N621 to Urdon.
DIFFICULTY: Strenuous to tough.
HIGHEST POINT: Horcada de Don Carlos 2422m (7946ft).
TREK STYLE: Mountain huts and hotels.
MAPS: Ediciones Adrados 1:25 000 Macizo Occidental, Macizo Central y Oriental.
FURTHER OPTIONS: Ascents of Morra de Lechugales 2441m (8009ft), Torre de Cerredo 2648m (8688ft) and Torre Santa de Castilla 2596m (8517ft).

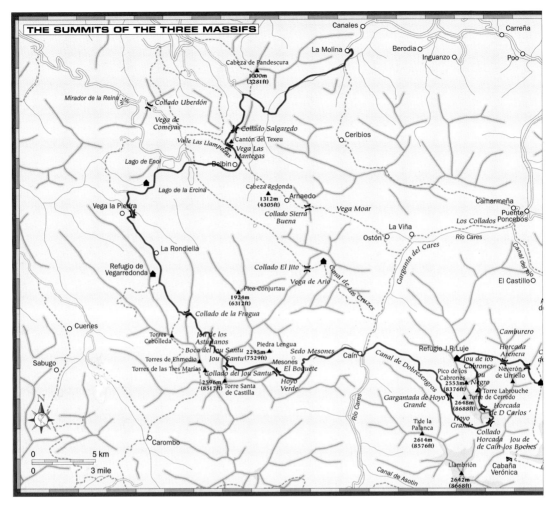

THE SUMMITS OF THE THREE MASSIFS

You will now begin to gain height, gently at first. Once you have entered the Cerrosa gully, however, a series of ascending zigzags over scree enable you to gain height rapidly. The next section, cut into the vertical walls above the gully, vertiginously leads up to La Bargona, a natural balcony that provides views over the whole of the gorge with the river some 300m (985ft) below. From the balcony,

the gradient eases off somewhat. Continue up through a series of long hairpins, one of which, known as Balcón de Pilatos (Pilate's Balcony), has a more or less 500-m (1640-ft) vertical drop off the side. At the top of the hairpins lies the village of Tresviso.

Tresviso has a special political status that allows it to have its own council, courts etc., not

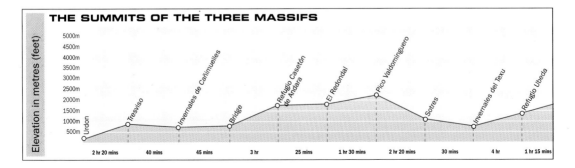

THE SUMMITS OF THE THREE MASSIFS

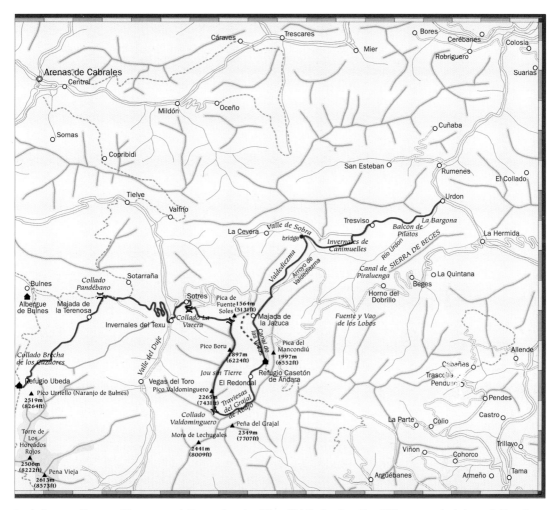

bad for a village with a population of only 35 people and which pre-1991 was only accessible by 4 x 4 or by foot. You can stay in the small hotel or the adjoining bunkhouse.

Tresviso to Refugio Casetón de Andara

From Tresviso take the tarmac road that leaves the village in a westerly direction and about 100m

(110yd) after the little car-park, take a left onto a jeep track. Follow this for a mere 10m (11yd) before taking a footpath off to the right – in summer, if the grass has not yet been cut, this path is quite difficult to locate. The path soon becomes more obvious and descends through open countryside with numerous types of butterfly, including swallowtails, fluttering around. After about 10

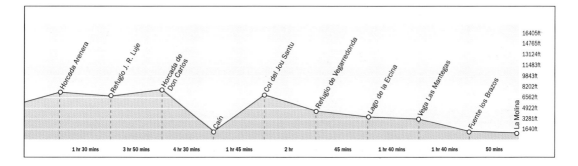

minutes the path is bisected by a jeep track, but the way on is straight ahead (marked with paint).

Continue down through woodland, eventually emerging into a lush pasture where the path disappears. Go straight across the field and, on reaching the other side, turn right to pick up the path again. Descend steeply on a zigzagging path through a forest and you will emerge in a clearing, Invernales de Cañimuelles. On the other side of the pasture are two somewhat dilapidated barns – the path goes directly between these barns. After about 150m (165yd) the obvious path starts to descend, however, you must take the vague, overgrown path that goes off to the right. After 20m (22yd) cross a little cliff on a narrow ledge – there are impressive views of the thundering river below.

Once on the other side of the river, the route becomes wider. Traverse the hillside on an undulating route of mixed terrain; despite being so near to Tresviso there is always a feeling of isolation on this section and care should be exercised, especially in misty conditions, as the route is not entirely clear. About 1 hour from the ledge cross the Río Urdon on a little stone bridge

PEAK: TORRE DE CERREDO

CLIMB ESSENTIALS

SUMMIT: Torre de Cerredo (Normal Route) 2648m (8688ft).
CAMP: Refugio Ubeda.
GRADE: Rock climb PD.

An ascent of Torre de Cerredo, which marks the highest point in not only the Picos de Europa, but in the whole Cordillera Cantábrica, is a must for anyone visiting this isolated zone of the Central massif. From the summit, you have excellent views of the Central and Western massifs and to the north the rugged coastline of the Bay of Biscay. For anyone walking in the Central massif it is an obvious target, as it presents no great technical difficulties in its ascent. It might be necessary to carry an ice axe, as the Jou de Cerredo can be full of snow until July.

From Refugio Ubeda head to Horcada Arenera col, you will see Torre de Cerredo to the south-west. Follow a vague path south-west in the direction of the summit until you near the base of the mountain in the Jou de Cerredo. From the Jou de Cerredo ascend diagonally across broken ground to a short, steep gully on the south-east face, which rises to the right. Climb the gully and, on exiting, climb diagonally left across easy slabs and ledges to the summit. Care should be taken to not dislodge loose rocks, especially if another party is below. The summit is marked with a concrete post, and note the excellent views down into the Cares Gorge to the west.

Descend via the same route.

Torre de Cerredo is the highest point in the Picos de Europa.

The peaks of the Western massif often remain snow-capped until mid-summer.

just below the defunct Sobra dam. Follow the path that goes south up the right-hand side of the Valdediezma valley at half height. After passing through a small beech forest the route emerges onto a good jeep track, which connects the villages of Sotres and Beges. Turn to the right and follow the track which, after passing two flat grassy areas, starts to climb steeply.

From this track there is a choice of how to proceed. The first and by far the easier option is to follow the track all the way up to just before the tarmac road and then take the track that goes up to the left and follow it without problem to Refugio Casetón de Andara. The other more complicated, but more rewarding option, is to take the vague footpath the leaves the track on the left of the second hairpin.

This option follows the footpath across a field, then crosses a small gully and climbs the muddy slope on the other side. Go steeply up to the right and, after going diagonally right, across some boulders, rejoin the gully. Now follow the valley up, without complications, until you reach a point where the way on is blocked by a small cliff. Looking back to the right a path can be seen ascending through the woods, take this path. You will soon gain open land. Pass the Majada de la Jazuca before continuing up the Canal de las Vacas. Eventually you will join the jeep track next to the Refugio Casetón de Andara.

Note: If it is misty, it would be advisable to leave out the first section of the day as far as the Sobra dam. The dam can be reached by following the road from Tresviso for some 2km (1⅓ miles) until, just after a little pass, a jeep track descends to the left all the way to the dam.

Refugio Casetón de Andara to Sotres
From the hut turn immediately right and due north. Very quickly the path doubles back and goes above the hut and gains a flat area. From here, take a path due west and descend slightly into the Andara lake depression. After about 10 minutes the path splits and the way on is to the left, walking round the side of what was once a lake but, due to a mishap during the mining era, is no longer there. A miner, so the story goes, apparently somehow managed to puncture the bottom of the lake. All the water now drains into the mine and on to a connecting cave system. Its waters emerge from the depths at one of the Picos de Europa's most spectacular caves, La Cueva de Agua, some 5km (3 miles) away. Ahead are some huge boulders; on closer inspection you will notice that these boulders have little houses excavated below them, complete with numbered doors. This disused settlement is called El Redondal and was once used by the shepherds from Tresviso.

Continue on the vague path, which now turns to the south. The path soon disappears and it's necessary to climb scree until you reach the Traviesas del Grajal de Abajo path some 200m (650ft) higher up. Turn right onto the somewhat collapsed path and follow it to Collado Valdominguero where a steep ramp gives access to the peak of the same name (2265m/7431ft).

From the summit the descent is across a short tricky ridge to the north and then into a shallow rock-strewn valley which passes round the side of the Jou sin Tierre depression before continuing down past Pico Boru and on to Collado Fuente Soles. From the col take the rocky path west down to Sotres.

Sotres to Refugio J. R Luje

Leave Sotres on the main road and, after descending for about 10 minutes, take a jeep track off to the left. Follow this track until you reach a junction by the barns of Invernales del Texu – turn right here. Follow the track up to another junction; turn right again and head up to the car-park just before the Collado Pandébano. Looking towards the col, take the steep grassy slope up to the right, passing a good spring, to two small barns. Beyond the barns an obvious path goes to the col a short distance away.

From the col head south on a good path that soon leads to the Majada de la Terenosa, a summer settlement. In the first of the buildings it's possible to buy cold drinks and some famous Cabrales cheese. From the last of the huts the path becomes more rocky, but it is easily followed up to the Refugio Ubeda, below the base of the towering Naranjo de Bulnes (Pico Urriello).

Looking north-west from the hut you will see the north ridge of the Neverón de Urriello. A vague path marked with cairns indicates the route over slabs and scree to the base of the ridge. A wide ramp rising northwards gives access to a short chimney that emerges in the Collado Brecha de los Cazadores. Looking back is undoubtedly one of the finest views of El Naranjo.

Head south, staying on high rocky ground, and quickly pick up the path that traverses the scree slope below Neverón de Urriello. The route is marked with cairns and occasional splashes of paint and finally climbs to the Horcada Arenera col (2283m/7490ft). From this often windy location are views to the south-west of the Torre de Cerredo, the highest peak in the Picos de Europa.

A steep descent west, then north-west, trends up past a snow-plugged cave entrance to gain a wide col with an often snow-filled depression beyond. This depression is passed by either going down and then up the other side, or by traversing round its left-hand side, which involves some easy scrambling (the way is marked with paint). On reaching the other side an easy gully gives access to another depression, which has a tall, striped pole planted in the ground to mark snow levels.

The route goes past the pole and over broken slabs before reaching a shoulder from where another col can be seen. The obvious way on is to drop down and then climb back up, although it's actually quicker and easier to climb up a small ramp on the left and then traverse round the hillside before ascending another ramp to the col. From the col take the obvious path into the depression below; the Refugio J. R. Luje is just off to the right, up a short grassy hill. To the south is the Pico

CABRALES CHEESE

Spain has the second largest variety of cheese in the world (France has the largest). One of the most notable cheeses of Northern Spain is, without doubt, the world famous Queso Cabrales. This flavoursome blue cheese, often compared with Roquefort, is made from any combination of unpasteurized milk from cattle (*vaca*), sheep (*oveja*) or goats (*cabra*).

After the initial process of manufacture the cheese is dried and then transported in wicker baskets on donkeys to be matured in local caves. This process can take between three to eight months. A contributory factor in the flavour of the cheese can be accredited to the type of hay and flora eaten which is scythed from the lush meadows then fed to the cattle, sheep and goats. Other variables affecting the taste are cave altitude, temperature and humidity. Taste and strength differ greatly throughout the year and increase with age. The traditional methods of manufacture differ greatly between families and have been handed down over generations; these are jealously guarded secrets.

The highlight of the year is the Arenas de Cabrales cheese festival. This Bachanalian excess takes place, without fail, on the last Sunday of August. It is on this auspicious date that the cheese is judged and eaten in vast quantities along with local cider and regional delicacies. In preparation for this fiesta, 20,000 cheese rolls (*bocadillos*) are made and the after-effects are felt for several days!

There are similar cheeses in the Picos de Europa without the 'Cabrales' label which, in many cases, are equally as good.

de los Cabrones, which dominates the whole area and is reckoned by many to be one of the most beautiful peaks in Spain.

A 20-minute climb up a grassy slope to the west of the hut gives access to the Collado del Agua, with views down into the Cares Gorge way below and the lofty summits of the Western massif in the distance silhouetted against a setting sun.

Refugio J. R. Luje to Cain

Leave the hut and head south-east across the double depressions of the Jou de los Cabrones. Climb the gully that trends east and breaks out onto a pass between two depressions. Now head south up to another little col from where the trail ascends the north-east ridge of Torre Labrouche; down to the right is the Jou Negro.

Continue round the left-hand side of Torre Labrouche to enter the Jou de Cerredo depression. On the far side of the depression – to the south – is the Horcada de Don Carlos col, which is gained by continuing to traverse round the side of the depression on broken terrain, followed by a somewhat awkward climb up to the col. Descend on the other side of the col, trending right (south) across scree to the nearby Collado Horcada de Caín. Now

PEAK: MORRA DE LECHUGALES

From Refugio Casetón de Andara there are two ways to climb Morra de Lechugales. The most direct route is via the mining track that goes past the Pico de Grajal de Abajo and then Pico de Arriba. However, this route proves to be very complex in terms of route finding, especially in mist.

The more straightforward option is to head to Collado Valdominguero, from where a vague route over rock and scree leads first up the north-east and then north-

An easy scramble up the rocky clump that is Morra de Lechugales provides great views.

west slope of Pica del Jierru (2424m/7953ft). From the spacious summit of this peak, descend the slope down the south side to join a path marked with splashes of red paint (these are only visible when ascending). The route con-tinues south round the Hoyo del Evanjelista depression before ascending to a small col that separates Morra de Lechugales from La Silla del Caballo Cimero.

From the col, the route heads west across a somewhat vertiginously inclined slab for a few metres before ascending to a wide plateau right next to the block-shaped Morra de Lechugales. Looking at the peak, there is an obvious chimney that is easily climbed, and then the summit is only a few metres away. From the top there are classic views across to the Central massif and 2000m (6560ft) below to the south is the valley of Liebana.

CLIMB ESSENTIALS

SUMMIT: Morra de Lechugales (Normal Route) 2441m (8009ft).
CAMP: Refugio Casetón de Andara.
GRADE: Rock climb PD.

turn west and descend once again over scree to the unmistakable Hoyo Grande depression, which is crossed north-westwards to reach the Gargantada de Hoyo Grande.

From here the long descent of the Canal de Dobresengros gully begins. The trail descends on rocky terrain more or less down the centre of the gully until, after losing more than 600m (1969ft) in height, it is cut short by a cliff. The way on is over to the left, where a narrow and difficult gully – El Canalón – gives access to a small grassy cirque where water can be found. Pick up a path that leads down towards the Río Cares and shortly before reaching the bottom turn left through the Sedo Mabro and head onwards to Caín. Caín has plenty of hotels and a campsite.

PEAK: PICO URRIELLO (NARANJO DE BULNES)

Pico Urriello, situated in the heart of the Central massif, constitutes what can surely be regarded as the pinnacle of Spanish mountaineering. This giant limestone monolith has over 40 routes on its four faces, with grades ranging from D to ED+. The most difficult, Sueños de Invierno, required 69 days of continuous winter climbing. During the summer months, hundreds of climbers can be seen tackling some of Pico Uriello's classic routes, such as the Rabada/Navarro, La Murciana, Amistad con el Diablo or the South Face Direct. Information on the routes can be found either in the nearby refuge or in various specialized climbing guides on the Picos.

South Face Direct (First ascent by A. &J. Tomas 13 August 1944)
Approach: Leave the hut and take the rocky path that heads north-east round the northern side of El Naranjo. After about 15 minutes the route enters the steep Canal de la Celada gully, which you must follow for about 45 minutes until reaching the south face of the mountain.

Pitch One (15m, D): The route starts to the left of and below a large black overhang in the middle of the face. Long deep cracks descend from a large niche (abseil ring just visible). Climb the 'organ pipes' cracks trending right with difficulty to a stance in the niche. A number 3 or 4 friend could prove useful.

The South Face Direct route is the easiest ascent of El Naranjo.

Pitch Two (40m, D): Leave the niche traversing to the right and climb the water runnels that lead directly to a small stance at the start of a large dièdre. Various pegs and threads in place.

Pitch Three (30m, PD): Follow the corner straight up easily to the next belay ring.

Pitch Four (40m, D). Continue in the dièdre until the belay point below a slab with deep water runnels.

Pitch Five (40m, PD): Climb the runnels up the slab trending right towards the end to reach the amphitheatre and belay bolts.

From here, an easy scramble up a small gully reaches the summit ridge, and then on to the top where there is a tiny statue of the Virgin and a post box (very slow service)!

Descend via the same route.

CLIMB ESSENTIALS

SUMMIT: Pico Urriello (Naranjo de Bulnes) South Face Direct 2519m (8264ft).
CAMP: Refugio Ubeda.
GRADE: Rock Climb D

Wonderful sunsets are a prime feature of mountain treks, such as this one over Pico de los Cabrones.

Caín to Refugio de Vegarredonda

Take the path that goes up to the almost deserted village of Caín de Arriba. The hardest part of the trek now lies ahead of you. The trail goes up the ever-steepening valley, through numerous zigzags, to just below a rock barrier. A steep path carved out of the rock, known as the Sedo Mesones, heads north up a gully. From the top of the gully the route continues up a grassy slope, past the Mesones spring and then trends south-west to the grassy Hoyo Verde depression. From this point on, the rest of the day's trail ascends in a general north-west-erly direction and is hampered by numerous rocky projections which have to be surmounted.

Eventually, after an exhausting climb, the trail enters the Jou Santu, via El Boquete col. From the col, situated in the very heart of the Western mas-sif, there are views of the major peaks that sur-round the Jou Santu depression: Torre Santa de Castilla, Torres de las Tres Marias, Torres de Enmedio and, directly to the north, Piedra Lengua.

Cross the depression on loose scree and a somewhat vague path on the northern side of the *jou*. After passing through the Collado Jou Santu turn north-west. You will pass through the Boca del Jou Santu and then round the Jou de los Asturianos depression, where the path becomes more obvious. Pass through the Collado de la Fragua and descend steeply down into the Canal de Vegarredonda, which leads to the refuge of the same name.

Refugio de Vegarredonda to La Molina

From the refuge, reverse the route described on day 5 of trek 13 (page 111) down to Lago de la Ercina.

From the lake's car-park, walk east towards a low ridge. A faint path goes diagonally right to the top of the ridge and a jeep track descends the other side into a valley. Follow this track until it ends at the small summer settlement of Belbin, with its shepherds' huts and water trough.

Now head north-west up a grassy slope and pick up a cobbled path to reach another small ridge. The rocky path goes round to the right and starts to descend. When it levels out after 100m (110yd) turn north-west once again and enter a small grassy valley, at the end of which is another cobbled path that ascends. After 10 minutes the path levels out; it is most important that you do not take the path on the left that appears half-way up this cobbled path. Follow the cobbled path that passes round the bottom of Salgaredo peak on the right-hand side, across fairly level ground, until you reach a jeep track. There will be views of the Comella valley on your left and Cabeza Pandescura peak in front.

Follow the jeep track steeply down for about 30 minutes until you reach the second wide grassy pass, with views down into the valley on the right. Just after passing a sharp left-hand bend where the track levels off, take the small path that goes off to the right. (If water is needed there is a trough about 200m (220yd) further down the jeep track on the right-hand side.) A small white sign on the first tree on the right of the path says 'COTO PRIVADA DE CAZA' (Private Hunting). The dirt path continues through woodland and after a few minutes the path forks either side of a large beech tree. Take the right-hand downhill fork towards the valley bottom. Cross the small stream and continue on. After 5–10 minutes the river will become visible below.

Ahead is a pyramid-shaped peak and the trail now leads into another valley. Continue gently down to a junction. Turn right and head south downhill. After a few minutes take a left-hand fork. Shortly beyond, the path becomes vague in places. Soon the river can be heard below on the left and, after crossing another small stream, ascend briefly before heading down to the river. Cross the river on stepping stones 50m (55yd) upstream of where the path joins it. Follow the path alongside the river downstream and cross the third bridge (Puente Pompedro) over the deep canyon. Just beyond the bridge is a junction; turn left and ascend into the village of La Molina. Sadly, La Molina has no bar, so for refreshment you must march on to Canales or Ortiguero. Buses are available from Canales.

PEAK: TORRE SANTA DE CASTILLA

Torre Santa de Castilla is a particularly rugged peak.

CLIMB ESSENTIALS

SUMMIT: Torre Santa de Castilla (Normal Route) 2596m (8517ft).
CAMP: Refugio de Vegarredonda.
GRADE: Rock Climb AD.

The easiest route up Torre Santa de Castilla is via the Canal Estrecha.

From Refugio de Vegarredonda trek to the Collado del Jou Santu. From the col, traverse south and later south-west, following small cairns and gaining height until you reach the start of the Canal Estrecha, located at the base of a small amphitheatre surrounded by steep walls.

The true start of the Estrecha gully is some 30m (100ft) further up and is reached by climbing the fluted slabs, first up to the left and then traversing right. A short distance up, the gully splits. Take the left-hand option, which soon ends at a steep wall. Traverse left and then, after a hard move up, regain the gully, which is followed more easily to the Brecha Norte col. From the col, traverse left across the south side of the peak and climb a short but steep wall to gain the east–west ridge. Follow the ridge for about 50m (55yd) to a less-defined col. Cross onto the north face and traverse horizontally left to a short gully which you must climb, then continue left below the summit to reach another easy gully. Climb this to the summit ridge and then on to the top.

Although the path sounds complicated for route finding, there are splashes of yellow paint marking the easiest line of ascent. Descend via the same route, where it might be necessary to abseil in a couple of places (pegs in place).

PICOS DE EUROPA DIRECTORY

GETTING THERE

By air: Bilbao is the most convenient airport for the Picos de Europa. This airport is served by many different airlines including British Airways, Go and Iberia. The high season for tickets is July and August, Easter and Christmas. If you're booking quite far in advance, look out for cheap deals on Go.
British Airways: www.britishairways.com
Go Airlines: www.go-fly.com
Iberia Airlines: www.iberia.com

By train: Train services run to and from León, Oviedo and Santander, the main access points for the Picos de Europa. To confirm train times, contact:
Bilbao Train Station: C/Gurtubay 1; tel. 944 395077
Bilbao Termíbus station: tel. 944 395205
León Train Station: tel. 987 270202 (RENFE), 987 271210 (FEVE)
Oviedo Train Station: C/Urías; tel. 985 250202
Santander Train Station: Plaza Estaciones; tel. 942 210211
RENFE, Barcelona: tel. 93 4900202

By bus: There are regular services to Cangas de Onís from Oviedo, to Potes from Santander and to Posada de Valdeón from León. To confirm bus times, contact:
León Bus Station: tel. 987 211000
Oviedo Bus Station: Plaza Primo de Rivera 1; tel. 985 281200
Santander Bus Station: Plaza Estaciones; tel. 942 211995
ALSA Buses: tel. 985 969600
Palomera Buses: tel. 942 881106

ACCOMMODATION

Manned Refuges

Albergue de Barcena Mayor: tel. 908 186657
Albergue de Bulnes: 20 places; open in summer; tel. 985 845943
Albergue de Llanaves: tel. 659 024 565; email albergue@ erasmus.com
Refugio Delgado Úbeda: 96 places; open all year; tel. 985 925200
Refugio Marqués de Villaviciosa: 40 places; open all year; tel. 650 900760
Refugio de Vegarredonda (1410m/4626ft): 68 places;
open all year; tel. 985 922952
Refugio Vegavaño: 25 places; open in summer; tel. 987 740326/699 633244

Unmanned Refuge

Cabaña Verónica (2325m/7628ft): tel. 942 730007

TOURIST INFORMATION

Picos De Europa National Park Information Centre: Travesía de los Llanos, Posada de Valdeón; tel. 987 740549
National Park Vistor and Interpretation Centre: Avda Covadonga 43, Cangas de Onís; tel. 985 849154

Arenas de Cabrales: tel. 985 845284
Cangas de Onís: Plaza Avda Covadonga; tel. 985 848614
León: Plaza Regia; tel. 987 237082
Potes: Plaza Jesús del Monasterio; tel. 942 730820
Fuente Dé Cable Car Station: tel. 942 736610

EMERGENCY NUMBERS

Emergency Services: tel. 112
Mountain Rescue: Cuartel de la Guardia Civil, C/del Obispo 7; tel. 942 730007
Guardia Civil: tel. 062

Adventure trekking isn't all uphill slogs, it can often take in more gentle routes.

EL CAMINO DE SANTIAGO

Any book that describes trekking in Northern Spain would not be complete without a mention of El Camino de Santiago, otherwise known as or The Path of St James or The Pilgrims' Route. This route is not only one of the world's longest walking routes, but historically it is also the world's first commercial trek. El Camino de Santiago takes various roads, tracks and paths through France and Northern Spain all the way to the religious city of Santiago de Compostela, one of Galicia's few major population centres.

Pilgrims cross the medieval Magdalena bridge to Pamplona. This is only one of many ancient bridges that will be crossed in the course of the Pilgrims' Route.

TREK 16: THE PILGRIMS' ROUTE

The beginings of this trek date right back to the 1st century. The name Santiago comes from the apostle Saint James, who travelled to 'Finis Terrae' – 'The End of the World' – as it was called by the Romans, in north-western Spain to preach and convert people to Christianity. In AD44, after his work was done, Saint James returned to Palestine, where he was taken prisoner by the infamous King Herod. According to legend, he was flayed alive, had salt and vinegar rubbed into his wounds and was finally hanged. His body was secretly taken by his followers back to the north-west of Spain where it was buried in an undisclosed location near Iria Flavia, 20km (12 miles) south of Santiago.

Hundreds of years later, in 813, a hermit named Pelayo heard music in a forest and saw a shining light. This place was subsequently given the name Campus Stellae, 'Field of Stars', which later transformed to Compostela. On further investigation by Bishop Teodomiro in the 9th century, the tomb of the Apostle was discovered at Compostela, and King Alfonso II had a chapel built on the location. Later, in 844, in a battle with the Moors near Logroño (La Rioja), a knight bearing a white standard with a red Cross appeared and fought against the invaders. He was immediately

A statue of Saint James takes pride of place on the Baroque facade of the cathedral in Santiago de Compostela.

recognized as Saint James and given the name 'Matamoros' (Moor Slayer) and declared patron saint of the reconquest of Spain.

Over the following centuries, more and more pilgrims followed in the steps of Saint James along El Camino de Santiago to cleanse their sins and be freed from purgatory. The routes they followed were once old Roman trading routes known as the *voje ladee*, as they followed the stars of the Milky Way. For more than a thousand years, from many points across Europe, pilgrims entered France and then continued on to Santiago de Compostela, one of Galicia's few centres of major population, via several routes. The original chapel built by Alfonso II in Santiago de Compostela became, after many changes, the Catedral del Apóstol.

In the Middle Ages the Path of St James attracted hundreds of thousands of pilgrims a year. Today, in an increasingly secular world, El Camino is still incredibly popular, with approximately 30,000 pilgrims walking, biking or horseriding along the trail each year. However, it is likely that the majority of those who undertake this long-distance trek do so for the glorious countryside and culture to be found en route rather than for the remission of their sins.

Roncesvalles to Zubiri (21km/12½ miles)

Before starting the mammoth task ahead of you, it is worth spending some time in the striking village of Roncesvalles. Particularly worthwhile are trips to the Gothic Church of Santa Maria, the Romanesque Chapel of the Sancti Spiritus and the 13th-century Church of Santiago.

During the first day the route passes through the villages of Burguete and Espinal before climbing to the top of the Alto de Mezquíriz pass (955m/ 3133ft), where the 16th-century San Cristobal church is located. Inside the church is a magnificent 19th-century altarpiece.

The route continues to Viscarret, Lintzoain and Erro. After crossing the Alto de Erro pass (801m/

TREK ESSENTIALS

DISTANCE: The route described here is, without doubt, the most popular and is known as the 'Camino Frances' (French Route). The starting point, however, is in Roncesvalles in the Spanish province of Navarra. The total distance covered is 754km (451 miles).

ROUTE SYMBOL: The route symbol is a scallop shell, and many believe that in earlier times a shell was used to scoop drinking water out of the shallow streams that are abundant along the way. Over the centuries the shell became not only a practical recipient, but also as the scallopings on the back of the shell all converge to a single point, it seemed to represent all of the routes originating throughout Europe converging on Santiago de Compostela. The regularity of signs depicting the shell make route-finding easy, however, remember to keep an eye out for them.

WHEN TO GO: For many people the most important time to walk El Camino is in July, with the aim of arriving in Santiago before 25 July, when the city celebrates the fiesta of St James. If this is not so important to you, then the recommended time would be in spring or autumn. In August, the traditional Spanish holiday month, it's incredibly hot and crowded on El Camino. The winter months offer fantastic snow-capped vistas, although the walker must be prepared for cold weather.

PILGRIM'S PASSPORT: If you want to receive the *Compostele* (certificate of proof that you have completed the pilgrimage), it is essential that you take a Pilgrim's Passport with you and get it stamped along the way. This passport is also a requirement for staying in the pilgrims' refuges. The passport is available from the Abbot's Office in the abbey at Roncesvalles.

HOW TO GET THERE: The easiest way to reach Roncesvalles is to travel from San Sebastián (Donostia) on the A15 (N240), or from Jaca on the N240 to Pamplona. From the N240, take the N135 to Zubiri and then on to Burgete (Auritz), from where it's only a short distance, still on the N135, to Roncevalles.

ACCOMMODATION: Accommodation along El Camino varies from luxury hotels, such as the state-run paradors, to the somewhat basic pilgrims' refuges (*refugios*). Many of the hotels along the way are in fantastic buildings that were once hospitals for pilgrims and served not only as medical centres but also as hostels.

2628ft) El Camino finally arrives in Zubiri. Here can be seen the Puente de la Rabia bridge (Rabies bridge) – legend has it that if any animal suffering from rabies crosses the bridge three times it will be cured. Accommodation can be sought in either the lodging house or the hostel.

Zubiri to Pamplona (20km/12 miles)

Today the route goes through Liárraz and Esquízoz, and then onto Larrasoaña with its medieval bridge. Based in Larrasoaña is the Sociedad de Amigos del Camino, an organization that provides walkers with plentiful information about El Camino de Santiago and its history.

From Larrasoaña continue to Akerreta, with its 18th-century Church of the Transfiguration. Head through Zuriain, and onto Irotz. Cross the Río Arga on a beautiful Romanesque bridge before reaching the village of Zabaldica (500m/1640ft), where a visit to the Church of San Esteban with its image of Saint James is worthwhile.

El Camino now continues to Arleta, and a chance to see the Romanesque Church of Santa María. The next village is Trinidad de Arre, followed by Villava, Burlada and eventually on to Pamplona (449m/1473ft).

Pamplona has a cathedral famous for having one of the most beautiful cloisters in Europe. The city has many hotels, pensions and the

The scallop shell is the official sign of El Camino, and there are numerous stories as to its origin.

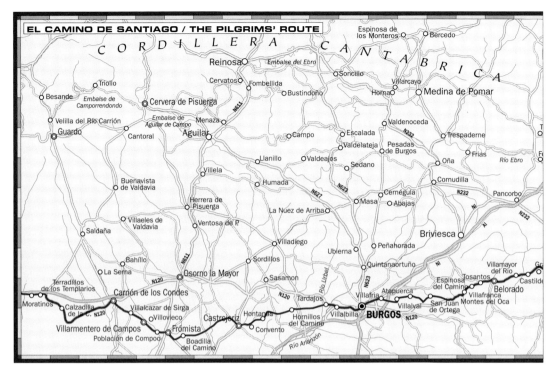

EL CAMINO DE SANTIAGO / THE PILGRIMS' ROUTE

Albergue de Peregrinos de la Parroquia de San Fermin. During your stay in Pamplona, make a point of visiting the Museo de Navarra, with its exhibition of Neolithic, Roman and Arabic cultures and remains.

Pamplona to Puente la Reina (25km/15 miles)
The third stage of El Camino begins in Pamplona and passes through Cizur Menor, where you can visit the 12th-century Iglesia San Miguel.

The journey continues through Zariquiegui (623m/2044ft). After crossing the Alto de Reniega pass (775m/2543ft) descend into the villages of Uterga, Muruzábal and Obanos (414m/1358ft), where an alternative route from Somport intersects with the Roncesvalles route beside the small Chapel of San Salvador.

The route now heads to Puente la Reina. This small town dates from 1090, and was named after the bridge built by Doña Mayor de Navarra in the 11th century. In the town there are several interesting churches worth a visit, including the Iglesia Santiago (12th century), which contains one of the finest multicoloured sculptures representing the apostle Saint James to be found anywhere along the route.

Puente la Reina to Estella (23km/13¾ miles)
Pilgrims should be getting into the swing of the trek by this stage. Leave the charming town of Puente la Reina via the medieval Puente de los Peregrinos. You will pass the ruins of the Bargota monastery before heading to Mañeru, with its many 17th- and 18th-century *palacios* (houses of noblemen).

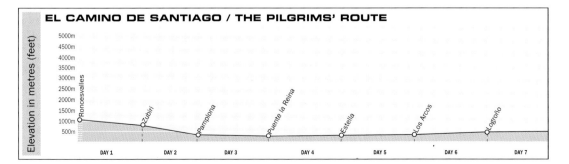

EL CAMINO DE SANTIAGO / THE PILGRIMS' ROUTE

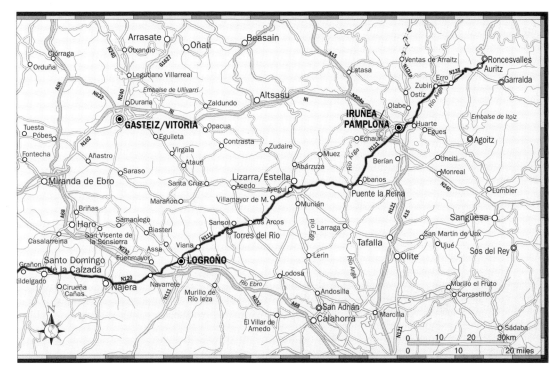

Journey on to the small medieval town of Cirauqui, which has a beautiful section of Roman road. Inside Iglesia San Román is a display of many mementos left behind by former pilgrims.

Cross an old bridge over Río Salado to Lorca, where the Romanesque Church of El Salvador, built in the 12th century, is located. Leaving the village behind the route enters Villatuerta, with its Romanesque bridge and several small churches.

The day's journey finally ends at the medieval town of Estella, with its impressive Portilla de Castilla, said to be one of the finest examples of early medieval architecture on the route.

Estella, known as 'the small Toledo' was founded in 1090 by the then king of Navarra, Sancho Ramírez. The town offers numerous sights, including Iglesia San Pedro de la Rúa from

the 12th century, with its beautiful cloister; the 12th-century Church of San Miguel, with its marvellous late-Romanesque facade; the Church of the Santo Sepulcro, also built in the 12th century and with a Romanesque facade; the oldest church in town, the 11th-century Gothic-style Church of San Pedro de Lizarra; and last, but not least, the Palacio de los Reyes de Navarra (Palace of the Kings), which also dates back to the 12th century.

Estella to Los Arcos (20km/12 miles)

The Path of St James now enters the municipality of Ayegui, where the Benedictine monastery of Irache, which is believed to date back to 958, is to be found. The monastery was once used as a hospital for pilgrims who arrived in Navarra on their way to Santiago, and in the 17th and 18th

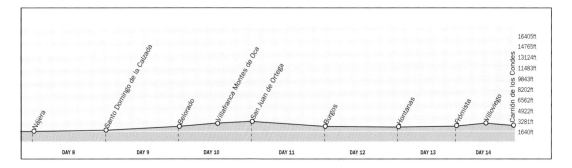

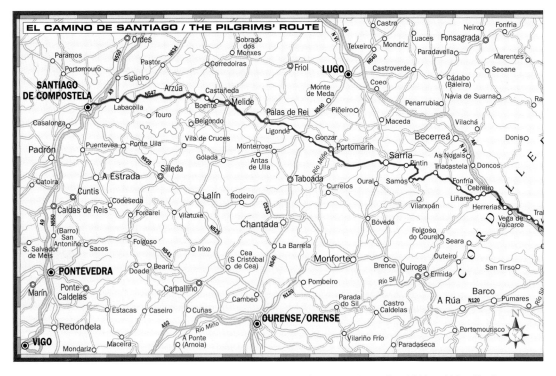

century became a university. Its interior houses Romanesque apses, ogival naves and a marvellous Renaissance Cloister.

Perhaps the highlight of a visit to this beautiful sanctuary, however, is the fountain that flows red with wine. And if you like the sound of this, be sure to make a trip to sample the wines at the Museum of Wine.

Leaving the monastery you must head for Azqueta, with its medieval fountain. Carry on to the 12th-century church and famous wine cellars of Villamayor de Monjardín. After passing through Urbiola, you will eventually come upon Los Arcos (447m/1467ft). Los Arcos is named after the arch found at the entrance to the village. In Iglesia Santa María is an image of the virgin which is illuminated by the rays of the sun on 15 June each year.

Los Arcos to Logroño (30km/18 miles)

From Los Arcos head for the municipality of Sansol and its 18th-century San Pedro Church. The route then heads for the village of Torres del Río, with its interesting Romanesque church built by the Order of the Santo Sepulcro in the 12th century.

After leaving Torres del Río, El Camino enters what was once a principality – Viana was established in the 15th century by Carlos III. Within this impressive walled town is the marvellous Renaissance facade of Iglesia Santa María, constructed between the 14th and 16th centuries. Its splendour is more characteristic to that of a cathedral, with five naves and 11 chapels. The interior has a lateral altarpiece dedicated to the memory of Saint James.

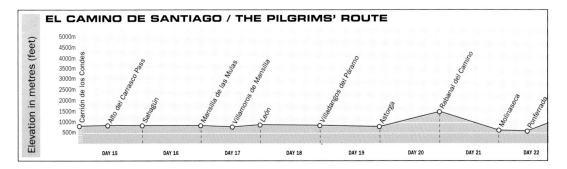

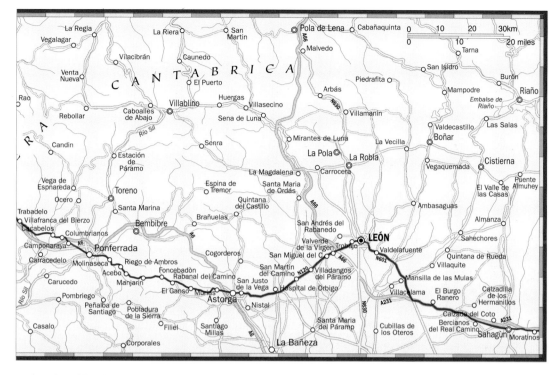

Leaving this charming town behind you will also leave the region of Navarra to enter La Rioja. After crossing an old stone bridge, Puente de Piedra, constructed by Alfonso VI over the Río Ebroyou enter Logroño, where you can spend the night.

The old quarter of the city still maintains its medieval atmosphere. The oldest two streets in the city (Rúa Vieja and Calle Mayor) have remained unchanged from a time gone by when many thousands of pilgrims passed by and used this town to replenish stocks for their arduous journey to Compostela. On the entrance to Iglesia Santiago is a 17th-century image representing the apparition of Saint James in the battle against the Moors at Clavijo in AD844.

Also to be found in the centre of town is the impressive Santa María del Palacio Church, which dates back to the 11th century and is distinct in that it possesses an impressively high 55-m (180-ft) tower. Also of interest is the Cathedral of Santa María la Redonda, which is crowned by two Baroque bell towers known as The Twins.

Logroño to Nájera (26km/15½ miles)

The next town along the way is Navarrete, which has an intact medieval main road. From here, the route moves on to Nájera, famous for being the birthplace of the Kings of the Pamplona–Nájera Kingdom. In 1030, Sancho el Grande changed the original route of the pilgrims to pass through this royal town. Soon after, his son Garcia IV built the Monasterio de Santa María la Real and a refuge, thus firmly establishing Nájera as a stopover for pilgrims.

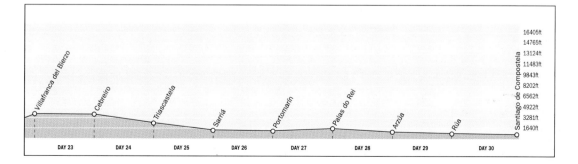

Nájera to Santo Domingo de la Calzada (22km/13¾ miles)

The journey now continues to the important San Millan de Cogolla sanctuary, the 6th-century Suso Monastery and the 11th-century Yuso Monastery. The Suso Monastery is believed to be the oldest community of its kind on the Iberian peninsula. It was here that the first words in the Castilian language were written, by a monk called Gonzalo. Also present are the remains of a pilgrims' hospital founded in the 12th century by Doña Isabel.

The route now continues through Cirueña and then onto Santo Domingo de la Calzada, which is often considered to be perhaps one of the most important stages of the Camino.

This striking city was named after a monk who was born in 1019 and who spent the greater part of his life dedicated to helping pilgrims by building and maintaining the paths. Domingo single-handedly constructed the bridge over the Río Oja. He also founded, not only a pilgrims' refuge, but also a hospital where he personally attended to the sick. It is said that despite the fact that there was no glass in the windows of the hospital, not one single fly ever entered the building and that the monk had the uncanny ability to not only cure the sick but also to revive the dead. For this Domingo was rewarded by being named a saint.

Three hundred years after Domingo's death the town's most famous miracle occurred. The story begins on a tragic note – a young man travelling the Pilgrims' Route with his parents was wrongly accused of theft and hanged. The parents, thinking their son dead, sadly continued on their journey to Compostela. On their return journey they were surprised to find their son still hanging in the town and actually talking to them to say he was alright. Somewhat shocked by this event they reported it to the local magistrate who was about to have lunch. He answered 'Your son is as dead as the chicken on my plate'. At this point, the chicken arose from the plate and started to crow. For centuries, these fantastic events attracted pilgrims who arrived in the city anxious to witness a miracle.

In Santo Domingo de la Calzada one can also find the luxurious Parador Nacional, which was constructed originally by Santo Domingo and later rebuilt in the 14th century.

Santo Domingo de la Calzada to Belorado (24km/14⅞ miles)

The ninth stage of the route leaves behind the province of La Rioja to enter Burgos. On the way to Grañón, pass by the Cruz de los Valientes (Cross of the Brave) commemorating the Juicio de Dios (God's Judgement). God's Judgement was a duel

The village of Navarette sits upon a hillside, and its narrow cobbled streets are great for wandering around.

The pilgrims' refuge at Santo Domingo de la Calzada is just one of an extensive network of refuges dotted all along El Camino Francés.

between a resident of Grañón and a resident of Santo Domingo over the ownership of a pasture. Martin Garcia from Grañón duly won, and is still to this day remembered as a local hero.

Continue on to Redecilla. Within the town's 14th-century Iglesia Virgen de la Calle is the San Lázaro Hospital for pilgrims. Head through Castildelgado, where there was once a monastery and hospital, before reaching Viloria, the birthplace of Santo Domingo. The next village on El Camino is Villamayor del Río and then the stopping place for the night, Belorado (772m/2533ft). Belorado is graced with a medieval spring, the Chapel of Nuestra Señora de Belén, the 17th-century Iglesia San Pedro Church and the 16th-century Santa Maria church.

Belorado to San Juan de Ortega (24km/14¾ miles)

Today the route passes through Tosantos, with its Chapel of Nuestra Señora de la Peña carved out of the hillside, then on to Villambistia, through Espinosa del Camino and on to Villafranca Montes de Oca, (950m/3117ft). Until 1075 Villafranca was the religious headquarters of the area and the residence of the bishops. The Iglesia Santiago was constructed on the site of a cathedral that was destroyed by the Moors.

Leave the town and pass through Valdefuentes to eventually reach San Juan de Ortega. This village marks the end of the day, and has a famous church built by a disciple of Santo Domingo.

San Juan de Ortega to Burgos (26km/15½ miles)

Pilgrims must now head for Agés and, on their way, they will pass the Chapel of Nuestra Señora del Rebollar (18th century). In Agés, where there were once iron mines, there is a small 16th-century church. The route leaves the village over a single-span Romanesque bridge and heads to Atapuerca, known worldwide for its prehistoric human remains that date back to over one million years. In the nearby Sima de los Huesos ('Shaft of the Bones') 32 skeletons have been uncovered that date back to 300,000 years ago. It is still not fully understood why these bodies were thrown down the shaft, but it is thought to be the oldest known burial ground in the world.

The path continues to Villalval and then Cardeñuela, from where it meanders alongside an old railway line as far as Villafría. From Villafría pass through Gamonal to finally reach Burgos.

Burgos (860m/2822ft) is a city that has long been connected with Saint James's pilgrimage. The magnificent Gothic cathedral, with its 84-m (276-ft) towers, is perhaps one of the most important in Spain and must be seen by any visitor to the city. Construction of the cathedral began in 1221, and it took 500 years to complete. The cathedral offers many attractions to visitors, such as the chapels of Condestable, Santiago and Cristo de Burgos, the choir, the facades and,

interestingly, the remains of the famous 11th-century Spanish soldier, El Cid, along with those of his wife, both of whom were brought here in 1921.

Burgos to Hontanas (31km/18½ miles)

After leaving the wonderful city of Burgos the route passes through Villalbilla and then, after crossing the Río Arianzon, Tardajos is reached, the origins of which are Roman. After crossing Río Urbel, El Camino arrives in Rabé de las Calzadas, before heading through Hornillos del Camino. Hornillos del Camino is dominated by an ogival church with three naves and a wonderful transept; the village also has two medieval bridges. The route continues on to Hontanas, the day's final destination.

Hontanas to Frómista (35km/21 miles)

The route for the 13th day of El Camino first goes past the 'Molino del Cubo' (a mill made from mud and straw) which is the first of many similar structures to be seen over the coming days. Pass the ruins of the 14th-century Convento de San Antón, where legend has it that pilgrims who were suffering from ergotism or St Anthony's Fire, a disease similar to leprosy, had the infected parts of their bodies amputated by the local Antonian monks.

Head towards Castrojeriz, the origins of which date back to an old Iber-Celtic castle which still dominates the town. After leaving the village you will enter the province of Palencia, and after crossing the Río Pisguera on the

The west front of Burgos's Gothic cathedral shows off the building's superb architecture.

The bell-tower of the church at Hontanas provides a good landmark for pilgrims trekking to this remote village.

Fitero bridge you will pass the little village of Itero de la Vega. During the Middle Ages, the inhabitants of this village had the unusual and remarkable right to elect their own lord.

The way on passes through Boadilla del Camino and then finally onto Frómista, another Celtic town, for the night. In Frómista the Romanesque Iglesia San Martín, which was once part of the now-destroyed Benedictine Monastery, houses several interesting stone sculptures. San Pedro's church and the Church of Santa María del Castillo (16th-century) are also worth a visit.

Frómista to Carrión de los Condes (21km/12½ miles)

Leaving Frómista behind, the route first goes through Población de Campos, where you have the chance to visit the fine 12th-century chapels of San Miguel and Socorro. The way on crosses the villages of Villovieco (814m/2671ft) and Villarmentero de Campos. The route continues on to Villalcázar de Sirga, with its 13th-century Iglesia Santa María la Blanca and 17th-century palace; the latter has been converted into a pilgrims' refuge.

Next you come to Carrión de los Condes, once an important medieval town that held court to many kings and queens. Worth seeing is the beautiful Romanesque facade of Iglesia Santiago, which is all that remains after the rest of the build-ing was destroyed by the French during the War of Independence in 1811.

Carrión de los Condes to Cueza to Sahagún (37km/22 miles)

Today's walk is quite long, but it could be split over two days using Calzadilla de la Cueza as a stopover. The first section to Calzadilla is unusual in that it covers quite a long distance without passing through the now customary villages.

From Calzadilla the route passes by the Santa María de las Tiendas church and then the village of Ledigos with its typical round-shaped mud-and-straw pigeon houses. From here, you must hike to Terradillos de los Templarios, Moratinos and San Nicolás del Real Camino. In the 12th-century the latter village was the location of a leper colony. The route now leaves the region of Palencia and enters the province of León at the Alto del Carrasco pass (865m/2838ft).

Descend into Sahagún – this historical market town was once home to one of the most important monasteries to be found in the north of Spain. The San Facundo monastery was one of the largest monasteries to be found along El Camino and was well known for its Mudejar (Muslims permitted to live under Christian rule) architecture. Today, all that remains of this beautiful building are a few walls. Also in the town is the operational Santa

Sahagún is rich in architecture – this view to the tower of San Tirso, a fine example of Mudejar architecture, takes in a Cluniac arch.

Cruz Convent, which dates back to 1546 and is run by Benedictine nuns who will provide accommodation to pilgrims as long as they are prepared to go to mass. The convent also houses the Municipal museum, with some fine works of art. The annexed church of Santa Cruz holds the remains of King Alfonso VI along with four of his six wives. Five kilometres (3 miles) south of the town is the national monument of San Pedro de las Dueñas monastery.

Sahagún to Mansilla de las Mulas (39km/23¾ miles)

After leaving Sahagún, the route advances towards Calzada del Coto, but just before reaching the village the route splits into two. The 'Camino Real Francés' goes south and passes through Bercianos del Real Camino, El Burgo Ranero and the tiny village of Reliegos; while the 'Via Trajana' – an old Roman path that is less busy and, therefore, perhaps the nicer option – heads north and passes through Calzadilla de los Hermanillos.

The two paths converge in Mansilla de las Mulas – a walled town dating back to 1181 that used to have seven churches, although today only two are in use. This will be the stopover for the night after a long day, whichever route option is taken.

Mansilla de las Mulas to León (21km/12½ miles)

Start the day by passing nearby Lancia, once one of the most important settlements of the Astures, who were beaten and then enslaved by the invading Roman armies after a fierce battle in Lancia in the 1st century. The route continues on to Villamoros de Mansilla (795m/2608ft). After crossing Puente de Villarente, which, with its 20 arches, is the longest bridge on the entire route, you enter the village of the same name.

From here, continue to Arcahueja, Valdefuente and finally León. León is one of the most important medieval towns in the whole of the Iberian peninsula, and home to such treasures as the Romanesque church of Santa María del Mercado, the Santa Ana Church, the Botines House designed by the eclectic and acclaimed architect Antonio Gaudí (1853–1926) and constructed around 1892 and, last but by no means least, the Gothic cathedral which is considered an architectural masterpiece.

León to Villadangos del Páramo (20km/12 miles)

On leaving this historic town the views at last

This lonely hermitage chapel is to be found near the village of Bercianos del Real Camino, which also has a fountain for thirsty pilgrims.

change from the somewhat monotonous horizons of the Meseta to the more rugged landscapes of the Cordillera Cantábrica mountains in the north.

Trek to Trobajo del Camino with its small chapel, and then to the La Virgen del Camino shrine. This shrine took over 450 years to complete; it was started in 1506 by a shepherd who claimed an apparition of the Virgin ordered him to build a shrine, which he immediately set about doing, however, it was not completed until 1961.

Continuing on, head through Valverde de la Virgen, then San Miguel del Camino, where there once stood, in the 12th-century, a hospital for pilgrims. Finally, aim for Villadongos del Páramo, where you can spend the night.

Villadongos del Páramo to Astorga (26km/15½ miles)

Although your legs are probably very weary now, push on to San Martín del Camino. After crossing the second longest bridge en route, which is well preserved, enter Hospital de Órbigo. It was on Pente Órbigo between 10 July and 9 August 1434 that one of Spain's famous knights, Don Suero de Quiñones, and nine of his chums jousted with 727

other knights from around Europe to prove his love for his lady friend Doña Léonor de Tova. It was said that anyone wishing to cross the bridge would have to fight him or cross the river by swimming. Anyone choosing the second option was immediately branded a coward. During the tournament only one person died and that was accidental, but it is said that over 300 lances were broken.

Unfortunately for Don Suero it was all to no avail, as Doña Léonor rejected him anyway. In response he went on a pilgrimage to Compostela, where he donated a golden bracelet (presumably an unwanted gift to Léonor) to the Saint. This bracelet is now on display in the cathedral. Don Suero died 24 years later in a tournament at the hands of one of his previously defeated challengers, Don Quijana.

The next village along the way is San Justo de la Vega. After crossing a Roman bridge you will enter the beautiful town of Astorga. This historical walled town was founded in 25BC and marks the convergence of the Camino Frances with the Vía de la Plata that comes from Andalucia. The town not only boasts a fine Gothic cathedral, but also another example of the work of architect Antonio Gaudí,

Superlative statuary forms the west porch of León's Santa María de la Regla cathedral.

Head on to rejoin the official Camino and continue on to Santa Catalina de Somoza. After passing through El Ganso, with its thatched roof houses and the remains of a Roman gold mine, you will reach Rabanal del Camino (1156m/ 3793ft), your home for the evening.

Rabanal del Camino to Molinaseca (25km/15 miles)

Leaving Rabanal del Camino, make your way into the more or less deserted village of Foncebadón. In the Middle Ages this was an important centre, as the next section of the route crosses mountainous terrain and in times of bad weather it would have been necessary to wait at Foncebadón until the weather improved. The next section goes over Monte Irago and Cruz de Ferro (1510m/4954ft), named after the iron cross that is mounted on top of a pole sticking out from a huge cairn. The cairn has been gradually built by stones placed by passing pilgrims – it is still tradition to add a stone as you pass. This peak is also important in that the Romans dedicated it to Mercury, the protector of the paths.

Pass through the abandoned village of Manjarín, with fantastic views of the surrounding landscape and on to El Acebo, where the curiously named Fountain of the Trout can be found. Continue through Riego de Ambrós and on to the final village for the day, Molinaseca, after crossing the Río Meruelo on a Romanesque bridge. Just before entering the village you will spot the Ermita de la Quinta Angustia. Molinaseca is famous for reputedly having the best chorizo sausage on the whole route, so be sure to buy some for lunch the next day.

Molinaseca to Villafranca del Bierzo (31km/18½ miles)

Take in the pretty village of Campo before reaching the important town of Ponferrada (541m/1775ft). This town, which dates back to Roman times, takes its name from the bridge that was constructed in the 12th century, La Pons Ferrata, meaning that it had iron banisters. It was almost 700 years before anyone had the idea of repeating

the Episcopal Palace. Gaudí's building replaced the original palace, which was unfortunately destroyed by fire in 1886. The Episcopal Palace houses the Museo de los Caminos.

Astorga to Rabanal del Camino (20km/12 miles)

The route leaves Astorga and the next town along the way is Valdeviejas, followed by Murias de Richivaldo. From this point the true Camino goes on to Santa Catalina de Somoza, but an interesting diversion is to pass through Castrillo de los Polvazares, which has a fascinating architectural history. The town was founded by the Celts and later occupied by the Romans who had discovered the existence of gold and extracted it from opencast mines. The remains of their presence can still be seen to this day. After the Moorish invasion, the village became deserted but was repopulated in the 9th century by people from Asturias, Galicia and Bierzo.

this form of construction (1779 in central England).

Also at Ponferrada is the 16th-century Sanctuary of Nuestra Señora de la Encina, which was constructed after the discovery of an image of the Virgin that had been hidden in an oak forest during the Moorish invasion.

Leaving Ponferrada behind, the route enters Columbrianos, with its interesting ancestrial homes, before reaching Fuentes Nuevas and then Camponaraya, with its many beautiful houses, one of which belonged to the bridge-jousting knight, Don Suero de Quiñones.

Head on to Cacabelos, with its Chapel of San Roque and also the church of Nuestra Señora de la Plaza. The inhabitants of this village were said to have been so tired of pilgrims asking stupid questions, that they asked King Alfonso IX in 1209 to change the route, but he declined to do so. El Camino then goes through Pieros and finally onto Villafranca del Bierzo, which was founded in the 13th century and where it is worth visiting the castle constructed by the Marquis of Villafranca in 1490.

Dusty tracks and a hot sun are common features of El Camino in the summer months.

Villafranca del Bierzo to Cebreiro (31km/18½ miles)

El Camino now passes through the medieval municipality of Pereje and then onto Trabadelo, which once belonged to the Church of Compostela after being donated by Alfonso III. The next village is Vega de Valcarce (636m/2087ft); here can be seen the remains of the 11th-century Castro de Veiga Castle, along with the nearby castle of Sarrac'n which dates back to the 14th century, and which was allegedly visited by King Carlos V in 1520.

The route passes the Ruitelán church and later the Chapel of San Froilán. Legend has it that San Froilán, who was later to become the bishop of Leon, was on his way to Lugo when he stopped here for a rest and along came a big bad wolf and ate his lunch. The cleric was so angry

that he made the wolf walk all the way to Lugo carrying his things.

A little further on is Herrerías, named after the many forges that were once found here. Trek on to La Faba, the only village on the route that has the church situated below the main part of the village.

The route finally enters the province of Galicia after passing through the last village of León province, Laguna de Castillo (1170m/3839ft). Not far away is the destination for the night, Cebreiro (1295m/4249ft) with its traditional thatched conical buildings, known as *pallozas*, whose origins date back to pre-Roman and possibly Celtic times.

Cebreiro to Triacastela (21km/12½ miles)

The first part of the route across Galicia goes through Liñares. After crossing the Alto de San Roque pass (1295m/4249ft) on the Sierra de Rañadoiro the route descends to the Hospital da

Condesa, which takes its name from the Countess Doña Egilo who founded the hospital at the end of the 11th century.

Next are the tiny hamlets of Padornelo and Fonfría, which are separated by the Alto do Poio pass (1337m/4387ft). The route passes through Viduedo, situated in a lovely setting which boasts the smallest chapel anywhere along El Camino, San Pedro. Continue through a succession of small villages: Filloval, Pasantes and Ramil, before reaching your destination for the night, Triacastela (671m/2202ft), which was founded in 922. Its name comes from the fact that there were once three castles (Tres Castillas). An unusual feature is the special prison for pilgrims that still contains incriptions left by wayward pilgrims over the last thousand years.

Triacastela to Sarriá (20km/12 miles)
The first port of call today is Balsa, with its tiny chapel of Nuestra Señora de las Nieves. The next section goes through a picturesque oak and chestnut forest to San Xil (865m/2838ft). The route then ascends over the Alto de Riocabo pass (910m/2928ft) before descending down to Montán, complete with Romanesque church. Next come several small villages: Fontearcuda, Furela, with the San Roque chapel, Pintín, Calvor, Aguiada, San Mamed, Carballal, Vigo de Sarria and finally, after crossing a bridge, Sarriá.

Sarriá is a reasonably sized market town, perhaps best known for the fact that on 23 September 1230 King Alfonso IX died here while making his pilgrimage to Santiago. After his death, his remains were taken to Santiago so that he should complete his journey and be buried alongside his father Fernando II. Among the medieval streets to this pretty town is the church of El Salvador with its Gothic facade; the hospital of San Antonio, which today is used as a court house; and the remains of a 14th-century castle and a monastery.

Sarriá to Portomarín (23km/13¾ miles)
Leaving Sarriá behind, the route goes over the river and onto Vilei. Barbadelo follows, with its 12th-century church of Santiago that has been declared a National Historical Heritage for its fine rural Galician Romanesque architeure. Of interest are the pre-Romanesque carvings around the doorway and windows, along with an interesting array of mythical creatures on the capitals. For the rest of the day the route passes through numerous villages surrounded by lush farmland, where the locals are only too pleased to stop for a chat with a weary pilgrim. The most important place along this section is Parrocha and its Monastery of Loio, the birthplace of the Knights of the Order of Santiago.

Eventually you will reach Portomarín, which dates back to Roman times. The current location of the town is not its original setting, due to the fact that in 1956 the valley in which it stood was flooded to provide power to a hydro scheme. Many of the important buildings were dismantled and moved stone by stone to its new location. When water levels are low, it's still possible to see the old bridge that used to cross the Río Miño.

Worth visiting is the church-fortress of the Knights of St John of Jerusalem – the 13th-century church of San Nicolás – and the portal of the church of San Pedro. This late 12th-century portal, was salvaged and now resides as the entrance to the town hall.

Portomarín to Palas do Rei (24km/14½ miles)
El Camino continues to head across Galicia and once more the scenery is one of rolling hills and green fields. The first of the many hamlets to be found in the area is Toixibó followed by Gonzar (560m/1837ft), Castromaior and Hospital da Cruz. Further on, the route enters Ventas de Narón, which was an important medieval town where pilgrims would rest before setting off across the Sierra de Ligonde. In 820, this was the scene of a crucial victory for the Christians in a bloody battle against the Arabs. The route continues on through Prebisa and then Lameiros, with its Chapel of San Marcos.

Descend into Ligonde, where Carlos V and Felipe II once stayed on their pilgrimage to Santiago and where there is an important pilgrims' graveyard next to the church.

Continue through Airexe, whose church has some interesting carvings: in between the two lions and a raptor is a human figure thought to represent the prophet Daniel.

Later, the route goes through Portos, from where a short detour permits pilgrims to visit Vilar de Donas with its fine Romanesque church of San Salvador. Now a national monument, the church was established in 1184 by the Knights of the Order of Santiago, whose role was primarily to fight the Moors, although in reality they spent more time

El Catedral del Apóstol in Santiago de Compostela is the final destination. Once there, many pilgrims undertake certain rites to formally complete their journey.

Weary feet will be unavoidable on the Pilgrims' Route. However, at Itero del Castillo the waters of the spring are said to have healing powers – two pilgrims try them out.

ridding El Camino of bandits. After returning to the main route you will pass through Lastedo, Valos and Rosario. The latter village got its name from the fact that on a clear day the city of Santiago can be seen for the first time and exhausted but excited pilgrims would stop here to say a rosary.

The way on continues to Palas do Rei, where you can spend the night. This town takes its name in memory of the Visigoth King Witiza who lived here from 701–709.

Palas do Rei to Arzúa (29km/17⅘ miles)
Not far to go now. The route leaves Palas do Rei and heads off in the direction of the province of La Coruña. You first cross San Xulián do Camino, whose small Romanesque church has an interesting transept.

The route passes through various hamlets before following a well-preserved section of the old Roman path. After crossing a medieval bridge the larger town of Melide, the geographical centre of Galicia, is reached. This important town marks the point where the northern coastal route joins the Camino Francés. The present parish church was the former headquarters of the brotherhood of Sancti Spiritus and contains stately sepulchres. Also to be seen is the Romanesque church of Santa María de Melide which dates back to the 12th century.

Continue on to pass through Carballal, Ponte das Peñas, Raído, Bonete and Castañeda, where the lime ovens used during the construction of

the cathedral in Santiago once stood. Historically, as a penance, pilgrims used to carry lumps of limestone in their packs from the mountains near Triacastela to these ovens. A medieval bridge now takes pilgrims through Ribadiso and then onto the beautifully located Arzúa for the night.

Arzúa to Rua (18km/10¾ miles)
Pilgrims will start today full of excitement, knowing that the journey is nearly over and that tomorrow they will be arriving at their goal of Santiago de Compostela. The route takes the weary traveller past Pazo As Barrosas, where there is the small chapel of San Lázaro. Further on, the route passes through Reido, Calzada, Calle and Salceda, where a small monument has been erected in memory of a Belgian pilgrim who died here on 23 August 1989. The route then passes through Brea, heads over the Alto de Santa Irene pass (410m/1345ft) and through Santa Irene before finally arriving at Rúa (295m/968ft).

Rúa to Santiago de Compostela (21km/12½ miles)
At long last, the final day on the Pilgrims' Route has come. You are entering the last section of a 754-km (451-mile) trek across a complete mixture of Spanish countryside and encompassing many of the countless wonders provided by centuries of history.

The final part of the itinerary goes through Burgo, followed by Arca, San Antón, Amenal and San Paio. Further on, the route arrives at Lavacolla, which bizarrely translates as 'Clean Behind', as this was where pilgrims washed themselves and their clothes after many months on the road in order to make themselves presentable before entering the town of Compostela.

The next place between you and your final, final destination is the hilltop of Monte do Gozo. Historically, pilgrims would race each other to the summit. Also, it was from this point, that anyone who had undergone the journey on horseback, would dismount to complete the journey on foot. All that remains of the journey from here are the 4.6km (2¾ miles) to the sacred gates to the cathedral of Santiago (251m/824ft), the end of a magnificent journey across Northern Spain.

EL CAMINO DE SANTIAGO DIRECTORY

GETTING THERE

By air: Madrid is the most convenient airport for both Roncesvalles and Santiago de Compostela, the start and finish of El Camino de Santiago. This airport is served by many different airlines including British Airways, BMI British Midland and Iberia, Easy Jet and Go.

BMI (British Midland): www.britishmidlands.com
British Airways: www.britishairways.com
Easy Jet: www.easyjet.com
Go Airlines: www.go-fly.com
Iberia Airlines: www.iberia.com

By train: RENFE train services from Madrid Chamartín run to and from Pamplona (from where you can catch a bus to Roncesvalles) and Santiago de Compostela. To confirm train times, contact:
Pamplona Train Station: Avda San Jorge; tel. 948 130202/948 227282
RENFE, Madrid: C/de Alcalá 44; tel. 913 5623333
Santiago de Compostela Train Station: tel. 981 520202

By bus: There are regular services to Pamplona and Santiago de Compostela from Madrid, and from Pamplona to Roncesvalles. To confirm bus times, contact:
Madrid Bus Station: C/de Alenza 20; tel. 91 5530400 (Bus Continental to Pamplona)
Pamplona Bus Station: Avda del Conde Oliveto; tel. 948 223854 (La Montañesa buses to Roncesvalles)
Santiago de Compostela Bus Station: San Caetano; tel. 981 587700/981 589090 (ALSA buses to Madrid)

ACCOMMODATION
Pilgrims' Refuges
Roncesvalles: 68 places
Zubiri: 20 places
Larrasoaña: 34 places; kitchen
Pamplona: C/Ansoleaga 2; 30 places
Pente la Reina: 60 places; kitchen
Estella: 64 places; kitchen
Torres del Río: 40 places
Logroño: 60 places; kitchen
Naverrete: 20 places; kitchen
Nájera: 30 places; kitchen
Santo Domingo de la Calzada: C/Mayor; 50 places; kitchen
Grañon: 20 places; kitchen
Redecilla: 30 places
Belorado: 22 places; kitchen
Villafranca Montes de Oca: 18 places
San Juan de Ortega: 60 places
Burgos: 60 places
Tardajos: 12 places
Hontanas: 20 places; kitchen

Castrojeriz: 35 places; kitchen
Itero de la Vega: 12 places
Boadilla del Camino: 25 places
Frómista: 30 places
Villalcázar de Sirga: 15 places
Carrión de los Condes: 60 places
Monasterio de Santa Clara (Carrión de los Condes): 28 places
Calzadilla de la Cueza: 25 places; kitchen
Sahagún: 64 places; kitchen
Burgo Ranero: 30 places; kitchen
Mansilla de las Mulas: 26 places; kitchen
León: Madres Carvajalas, Plaza Santa María del Camino; 30 places; Edif. Antiguos Huérfanos Ferroviarios, Avda del Parque; 80 places
Villadangos: 50 places; kitchen
Órbigo: 20 places & kitchen (municipal); 30 places & kitchen (parish)
Santa Catalina de Somoza: 12 places
Rabanal del Camino: Refugio Gaucelmo; 40 places; kitchen
El Acebo: 10 places
Molinaseco: 30 places
Ponférrado: 80 places
Cacabelos: 60 places; kitchen
Villafranca del Bierzo: 40 places (muncipal); Refugio Jesús Jato: 40 places
Vega de Valcarce: 28 places
Cebreiro: 90 places; kitchen
Hospital de Condesa: 20 places; kitchen
Triacastela: 56 places
Sarria: Rúa Maior 79; 40 places; kitchen
Barbadelo: 20 places; kitchen
Portomarín: 100 places; kitchen
Gonzar: 20 places; kitchen
Airexe: 20 places; kitchen
Palas do Rei: 66 places; kitchen
Melide: 130 places; kitchen
Ribadiso: 60 places; kitchen
Arca: 80 places; kitchen
Monte do Gozo: 800 places
Santiago de Compostela: Seminario Menor de Belvís

TOURIST INFORMATION
www.xacobeo.es
Pamplona: C/Duque de Ahumada 3; tel. 948 220741
Roncesvalles: C/Ant. Molino; tel. 948 760193/948 760301
Santiago de Composteal: Rúa do Vilar 43; tel. 981 584081

EMERGENCY NUMBERS
Emergency Services: tel. 112
Guardia Civil: tel. 062

THE MOUNTAIN ENVIRONMENT

The limestone of El Frade in the Picos de Europa shines bright in the morning sun.

Geology and Origin

Northern Spain's oldest rock formations are found in the western part of the Iberian peninsula in Galicia, parts of Castilla–León and Extremadura. These consist of quartz and slate and result from the enormous forces at work when the masses of the Eurasian and the African continents moved some 500 million years ago.

During the Permian Convolution 280 million years ago, the Iberian peninsula was pushed up above sea level and the first mountain chains were formed. Over the next 50 million years or so, these old mountains became almost levelled by erosion from wind and rain.

Then, about 220 million years ago, the whole area sank, and the sea once again inundated the still young continent. The ocean floor became covered in a layer of clay, sand and limestone that was over a thousand metres thick in places.

During the end of the Mesozoic period, about 65 million years ago, the African continent collided with Southern Europe. Iberia once again surfaced and was slowly pushed into the European continent. It was during this period that most of the earth's mountain systems were formed, such as the Pyrenees and the Cordillera Cantábrica, as well as the Alps and parts of the Andes and Himalaya.

The last convolution was during the Eocene period 40 million years ago, when the Pyrenees and the Picos de Europa achieved their definitive appearance.

What is particularly interesting is that areas such as the Picos de Europa still have an annual growth of around almost 10cm, although due to constant erosion the net height gain is more or less zero.

Although there was massive glacial activity during the last ice age, all of these glaciers have almost completely disappeared.

MOUNTAIN PHOTOGRAPHY

MOUNTAIN PHOTOGRAPHY

The best way of recording your impressions of a trip to the mountains of Northern Spain is with a collection of photographs that capture those precious moments of scenic splendour. Few travel these days without a camera, but attitudes to photography vary from the casual to the complete obsessive. As you will be carrying your camera equipment for many days during a trek, some consideration should be given to both the type of camera chosen and the film stock used.

PRINT PHOTOGRAPHY

If all you require at the end of your trip is a set of prints to pass around your family and friends, then using a middle speed (100–200ASA) print film and having it processed by a normal commercial service should be adequate. In this case, a compact auto-focus camera with a zoom lens and built-in flash is ideal. There are hundreds to choose from, but for mountain and general outdoor use go for a waterproof or splash-proof model, as these tend to have rubber seals that also serve to keep dust at bay. If you are only going to process prints it is not really worth carrying a heavy professional SLR system unless you are prepared to pay for expensive specialist processing and printing. However beautifully you may monitor your exposures using the sophisticated exposure meter on a modern SLR – to capture particular features of a landscape, for example, or detail in a wonderful shadowy forest – all this will be lost when the film is processed and printed by a standard service. The modern machines used by such print-processing services simply take an average exposure value for the print. In practical terms this means that any scenes containing a high degree of contrast will be disappointing, with either sky detail washed out or foreground shadow lost completely.

SLIDE PHOTOGRAPHY

If you think you may want to give the odd slide show, reproduce some of your images for framing or even consider publishing the odd shot, you should opt for colour slides. The total contrast capable of being accurately rendered by a slide film is over ten times that which a print can reproduce. In a mountain environment, where scenes often include snow slopes, bright sunshine or valleys in deep shadow, the benefits of reversal or slide film are enormous. It is recommended to use a 100ASA or slower film. As slide film is developed by a set process, any subtle exposure variations made with the camera are faithfully reproduced in the final transparency.

A couple of other factors should be considered for slide photography. The exposure meters of most SLR cameras are calibrated for print film, and slide emulsions tend to be more sensitive. As a rule of thumb always underexpose slide film by or ⅔ of a stop – that is, shoot 50ASA film at 64 or 80ASA. This is only a very minor adjustment, but it does allow the film to produce maximum colour saturation. Each camera's meter is slightly different, so if you are taking your photography seriously, shoot a roll of your chosen film at home and bracket each exposure by up to two whole stops and observe the results. This will also give you a good idea of how the film handles over- and under-exposure.

CHOICE OF FILM AND LENSES

Choice of film always provokes debate. The faster the film (the more sensitive to light), the less capable it is of reproducing either colour saturation or contrast. Slower films are richer, sharper and have greater latitude. They also require more light to create an image, and in low-light conditions this can be problematic as your shutter-speeds decrease, introducing the possibility of camera-shake blurring the picture. The longer the focal length of the lens, the more pronounced this effect becomes, and for sharp hand-held exposures your shutter speed should be a value higher than the focal length of your lens in millimetres. Don't shoot slower than $\frac{1}{125}$ second with a 135mm lens. High in the Spanish mountains the light is often intense, and this problem only really occurs at dawn and dusk, but enthusiasts will want to be capturing just these times of day, thus the choice of lens is crucial.

The speed of film you choose will affect the type of lens you need. Assuming you want perfectly exposed, pin-sharp slides with rich colour saturation. Fuji's Velvia is an obvious choice, but it's only rated at 50ASA, and by the time you've put a polarising filter on your camera you've effectively reduced this to 18ASA. Most zoom lenses have maximum apertures in the f3.5–f5.6 range, and in low light, shooting slow film, you would be struggling with shutter-speeds of ¼ second or slower, which is way too slow for hand-held exposures. To allow yourself flexibility in these light levels, you should really use a faster lens (i.e. one capable of transmitting more light). Professional photographers always choose this option and use lenses with maximum apertures of f2, f1.8 or even f1.4 (and even then often in conjunction with a tripod). It is possible to buy faster-than-average zoom lenses, but they are prohibitively expensive. Almost 99 per cent of pictures taken with a zoom tend to be at one or other end of its range, where a zoom lens is at its least efficient. Carrying two or three fast lenses with fixed focal lengths akin to the extent of a zoom is recommended. Use a 28mm f2.8, a 50mm f1.4 and a 90mm f2 rather than a 28–80mm f5.6 zoom. You may have to think about your photography a little more, but your results will be vastly improved.

BATTERIES AND CAMERA CARE

Another key point to consider when choosing a camera for a trek is the type of battery required. In Northern Spain this is not as relevant (except when winter trekking or ice climbing) as in other mountain ranges of the world, such as the Himalaya, Andes or even the Alps. Modern auto-focus, power-wind cameras of all types rely totally on battery power to function. There is actually a strong argument for using vintage mechanical cameras. Alkaline cells perform very poorly in low temperatures, but a camera that runs on lithium

cells will be happily snapping away before dawn at 5000m (16405ft) when the thermometer is showing -25°C. All batteries drain more quickly at low temperatures, so keep them warm in your tent over night.

Dust, water and physical violence are the enemies of both photographic film and the delicate mechanisms inside every camera. Use a modern padded camera case, preferably one with a dust-gusset. Carry a blower-brush and lens tissues and use them meticulously. Clean the back of the camera every time you open it to change a film – the slightest specks of dust on the pressure-plate inside will give you skies bisected by perfect tram-lines. Heat and humidity ruin any kind of film, so carry yours in a proper waterproof bag – especially the exposed rolls.

TECHNIQUE

However many books you read, seminars you attend or friends you discuss it with, you'll only ever define your own photographic style and find out what pleases you by travelling with your camera, pointing it at the world and contemplating the results. Mountain landscape photography requires a certain element of technical accomplishment, but most of it is the result of the vision of the photographer.

This glacial lake and surrounding mountains are typical of the landscape in the Saint Maurici National Park.

One essential point to remember is that the definitive mountain photograph does not depend on form and composition, but on light – mountain light. In mountainous regions nature puts on a daily light show that often defies language to describe it. Most of the time it defies the photographer to capture it as well, but there are two 'magic hours', around sunrise and sunset, when colour and contrast and shadow combine to bring the contours of any vista alive.

HEALTH AND SAFETY

ACUTE MOUNTAIN SICKNESS

Although Acute Mountain Sickness (AMS) occurs normally above 3000m (10000ft) and is, therefore, not a significant problem in the treks described in this book, there have been recorded instances as low as 1800m (6000ft), so it is perhaps worth being familiar with the symptoms. AMS is brought on when a person ascends too fast for adequate acclimatization to take place, and is simply the collection of fluid between the cells of the body, or edema. This primarily occurs in two potentially dangerous areas – the lungs (high-altitude pulmonary edema or HAPE) and the brain (high-altitude cerebral edema or HACE). Initial symptoms may be mild and are not a reason to panic or disrupt an itinerary. Shortness of breath and a dry, hacking cough are early signs of HAPE, whilst headaches (especially on waking in the morning), loss of appetite and nausea are indicative of HACE. Other, less serious, signs of inadequate acclimatization are peripheral edema (swollen fingers, toes or face) and what is known as Chaine-Stokes respiration at night – when a sleeping person stops breathing for half a minute or so, and then takes several deep breaths before slowly tailing off again. The latter is more alarming for any person sharing the tent than it is dangerous, and the urge to shake the victim awake should be resisted. Religious adherence to three simple rules will prevent any drama or crisis due to AMS:

- Learn and recognize the symptoms of AMS and do not be afraid to communicate them to your companions.
- Do not continue to ascend while suffering any of the symptoms.
- Do not remain at the same altitude it your symptoms are worsening, even if it means descending at night.

BASIC MOUNTAIN FIRST AID

First Aid refers to the initial management of an injured person before they are taken to a doctor or hospital. In many of the remote areas of the Cordillera, a doctor or hospital could be over a few days' walk away. Knowing the basics of first aid, and being able to deal with an injury correctly in the first instance can often mean the difference between life and death, and can prevent the later development of life-threatening complications. In the event of an accident in which immediate action is necessary to save a life, the priorities are ABC:

A – AIRWAY B – BREATHING C – CIRCULATION

AIRWAY

Establish an open airway. Listen for breathing sounds and if there are none, lift the chin and jaw upwards, and tilt the head back. If there is an obvious foreign body blocking the airway, such as vomit or food, remove it. With any victim who has fallen from a height or received a head injury, be aware that they may have broken their neck and, if at all possible, do not attempt to move the patient. Keep the neck straight. In any situation where the airway is obstructed, however, the airway MUST take first priority.

BREATHING

Breathing patient

If, after clearing the airway, the victim is breathing, turn them on their side into the recovery position. The lower leg should be straight and the upper one bent at the knee to act as a stabilizer. Ensure that the airway remains open by continuing to extend the head, and tilt the jaw.

Non-breathing patient

Start mouth-to-mouth resuscitation: pinch the nose and blow into the victim's mouth. Form a tight seal with your own lips and watch their chest rise as you exhale. Perform two effective breaths before checking the pulse.

CIRCULATION

If the victim continues not to breath after two rescue breaths then check the pulse in their neck. If there is no pulse, start Cardio-Pulmonary Resuscitation (CPR). CPR is performed by placing the heel of your hand, with your other hand on top, on the middle of the victim's chest, two fingers' distance above the bottom of the sternum (chest bone). Press down to a depth of 4cm (½in), at a rate of 100 compressions per minute. After every 15 compressions give 2 rescue breaths, and continue at a rate of 15:2. Continue until the victim shows signs of life, until you are exhausted or until skilled assistance arrives.

Bleeding

If there is an obvious site of major bleeding,

attempt to stop the flow of blood by applying firm pressure directly over the site for at least 10 minutes without releasing pressure. Maintain pressure during evacuation as much as possible by applying a firm bandage and dressing. Do not remove during evacuation. If the bleeding is from a limb, then a tourniquet can be applied above the site of bleeding, taking great care not to over-tighten and stop the flow of blood to the limb entirely. Remember that not all bleeding is visible and the patient may be bleeding heavily inside their chest, abdomen or limb. Always remember ABC (see page 153).

Hypothermia

Do not forget that an injured person in extreme conditions will become hypothermic very quickly. Remove wet clothes, if possible, shelter from wind and rain and cover with emergency blankets, sleeping bag, etc. Lie down and cuddle the victim if all else fails. A person is not considered dead until WARMED AND DEAD. With a hypothermic person always continue resuscitation attempts (if possible) until the person is warmed.

Drowning

The priorities for a person who has been pulled from water are the same as for any unconscious patient – ABC (see page 153). Remember that they will also be hypothermic.

Choking

If the patient is conscious, bend them over forwards and carry out firm back blows. Encourage them to cough. If the back blows fail, then attempt abdominal thrusts (Heimlich manoeuvre) by standing behind the patient and placing both arms around the upper part of the abdomen. Clenching one fist and holding this with your other hand, pull sharply backwards and inwards. This will hopefully produce a sudden expulsion, causing the foreign body to be ejected from the airway.

It the patient is unconscious, then ABC (see page 153) are first priorities. An abdominal thrust can be tried by straddling the victim and pushing down into the upper abdomen with your two clenched hands.

Fractured Limbs

Any suspected fracture should be splinted as comfortably as possible using whatever means are available. Examples are tree branches, pieces cut from closed-cell mattresses (Karrimats),

Thermarests, pieces of wood, walking sticks or even better, a Sam-splint® . If the bone is sticking out of the skin then cover with a dressing and evacuate the victim. If evacuation is delayed then consider administering antibiotics, such as penicillin, to prevent infection. Straightening a badly deformed limb will help relieve pain and stop internal bleeding.

Dislocations

If a joint is obviously dislocated then it may be worth attempting to put it back in place, as this will help with pain relief. Administer adequate pain relief, then splint the limb as comfortably as possible and evacuate. If a limb below a dislocation is white, without a pulse and painful then this may mean that a major blood vessel to the limb is compressed. Such a limb is at risk of gangrene and the joint must be put back in place immediately if possible.

Lacerations and Cuts

The basic rule of thumb is that any cut older than six hours should not be sutured (stitched). If a wound is dirty and old, clean it thoroughly with antiseptic (povidone iodine is best) and cover with a clean dressing. Freshly cleaned recent cuts can be sutured or closed if less than six hours old. Consider using paper or 'butterfly' sutures. If there are signs of infection such as pain, redness and pus, then start a course of antibiotics, such as penicillin or amoxicillin.

Dehydration

If you suspect that a person is dehydrated, if possible give Oral Rehydration Salts (ORS). These should be given in small sips every 10 minutes to prevent vomiting. If there are no ORS available, a solution can be made by warming one litre of water and dissolving eight teaspoons of sugar and one teaspoon of salt. If the patient is unable to take oral fluids then intravenous fluids should be started. Evacuation will be necessary.

Confirming Death

A person is only deemed dead when there are no signs of life:
- No breathing
- No pulse
- Pupils are fixed (do not move when a light is shone) and dilated
- Hypothermia has been excluded

Glossary

abrigo = shelter
agua potable = drinking water
albergue = shelter/refuge
área de acampada = camping area
arroyo = stream/brook/creek

barranc(o) = gully/ravine
bocadillo = long sandwich
borda = summer mountain hut for shepherds
bosque = forest
brecha/brêche = breach/gap/opening

cabaña = hut/cabin/shack
camino = footpath/track/path/trail/road
casa rural = rural house/farm with rooms to let
cascada = waterfall/cascade
Circo/cirque/coma = bowl at head of valley
coll/collado/cuello/golada = mountain pass
cordillera = mountain range

dehesa = woodland pasture
desfiladero = gorge/defile/narrow mountain pass

embalse = river/dam
ermita = wayside chapel/hermitage
estanh/estanque/estany = pool/small lake/tarn

finca = building or section of land, usually rural
fuente = spring/fountain/water source

garganta = gorge/ravine
guía = guide

hito = cairn/landmark
hospital = hospital or wayside guesthouse
hospitalero = guesthouse or refuge attendant on El Camino de Santiago

ibón = small lake/tarn
iglesia = church

jou/hoyo = a hollow/depression
lago = lake
laguna = pool/lagoon
llano/pla/plan = plain
loma = low ridge

macizo = massif
majada = sheepfold/pasture
mapa = map
Meseta = high tableland of central Spain
mirador = lookout/viewpoint
mojón = boundary marker/large cairn
monasterio = monastery
montañero/a = mountaineer

nevero = permanent high-level snowfield

parque nacional = national park
parque natural = nature park/reserve
peregrino = pilgrim
pico = peak/summit
piedra = stone/rock
pista = trail/track
presa = dam
pueblo = village/small town
puerto/port = port/pass

rambla = seasonal water-course/avenue
refugi/refugio = refuge/mountain hut
río/riu = river
ruta = route

senda = path/track
sendero = footpath
serra/sierra = mountain range
sima = pothole/sink hole/fissure

teleférico = cable car/funicular
torrente = beck/mountain stream/narrow valley

vall/valle = valley
vega = pasture/meadow
vivac = bivouac

Bibliography

Angulo, Miguel: *Pirineos I/II* (1995), Donostia

Cabo, Roberto: *Reiseführer Natur/Spanien* (1991), BLV / München

Collomb, Robin G.: *Picos De Europa, Northern Spain* (1983), West Col Productions

Farino, Teresa: *Picos de Europa* (1996), Sunflower Books

Goyarrola, Fernando Obregón: *50 Rutas por la Cordillera Cantábrica* (1997), Edition Estudio/Santander

Goyarrola, Fernando Obregón: *Rutas por los Montañas de Cantabria* (1995), Edition Estudio/Santander

Lipps, Susanne: *Richtig Wandern/Pyrenäen* (1991), DuMont/Köln

Lucia, Paul: *Through the Spanish Pyrenees* (2000), Cicerone Press

Streatfeild-James, Douglas: *Trekking in the Pyrenees* (1998), Trailblazer

Walker, Robin: *Walks and Climbs in the Picos de Europa* (1989), Cicerone Press

Insight Guide – Northern Spain (2001), APA Publications

Walking in Spain (1999), Lonely Planet

INDEX

ACKNOWLEDGEMENTS

AUTHOR'S ACKNOWLEDGEMENTS

Specially dedicated to Gema for introducing me to the secrets of these valleys and mountains and for providing support and patience during all the hours of research in the mountains or in front of the computer. Further thanks goes to my parents and to all my friends in Anso and the Pyrenees. A special thanks to Toni and Marie Paz along with my many friends in the 'Posada Veral' and in Zuriza for their special help and warm hospitality.

Also, all my thanks to Manuel de Cos Fernandez and Marcos Cobo Rios for their help and companionship during the research of the Saja and Besaya National Reserve, and to Stephan Stolz for his advice on details of the Trashumancia.

Ilja Schröder

CONTRIBUTORS
Additional text contributors:

Dr Rachel Bishop and Dr Jim Litch (Health and Safety, pages 153–4)
Steve Razzetti (Mountain Photography, pages 151–2).

Additional photographic contributors:

M. A. Adrados (pages 125 and 126)
Gema Alonso (page 99)
Santiago Yaniz Aramendia (page 58)
Dr John Crook (pages 130, 133, 138, 139, 140, 141, 142, 143, 144 and 148)
Juan Carlos Muñoz (page 82)